HERE TO HELP!
(within reason)

John P. Hogan
HERE TO HELP! (within reason)

Insert Press, 2022

ISBN: 978-1-947322-05-9
Library of Congress Control Number: 2022934863

Thank you to CalArts for support of this publication through the CalArts Alumnx Graphic Design Seed Grant.

Concept: John P. Hogan & Dameon Waggoner
Cover & Layout Design: Dameon Waggoner

Essays:
John P. Hogan
Molly Jo Shea
Michael Ned Holte

Thank you to Adam Otto Lutz, whose (unofficial) *Official California Institute of the Arts Residency* was the impetus for this project. Special thanks to the many hardworking stewards of CalArts studios and galleries, past and present, including Clara Baxter, Danny Bengston, Abra Conn, Martina Onyemaechi Crouch-Anyarogbu, Greg Curtis, Elijah Ford, Luna Galassini, Amanda Galli, Liz Glynn, Sayre Gomez, Cory Hanson, Brennan Hill, Isabel Ivey, Aaron Johnson, Bryce Johnson, Jason Kunke, Scott Lee, Alejandra Lopez, Magnus Maxine, Ignacio Perez Meruane, Julian Prins, Ginger Quintanilla, Jorge Alexeis Reyes, Camellia Saleh, Connor Schwab, Grace Stott, Taralyn Thomas, Efrain Torres, Joshua Weinberg, Ben White, Angie Woolery-Herrera, Aaron Wrinkle, and Bedros Yeretzian. Love and thanks to Christina Ondrus, Jack Hogan, and Mike Hogan, for their support through the years, and particular gratitude to Auden and Liam, for the shining brilliance of their life force.

JOHN P. HOGAN

HERE TO HELP!
(within reason)

Studio Manager Flyers
California Institute of the Arts • 2006-2019

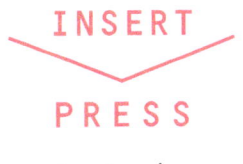

Los Angeles

INTRODUCTION
John P. Hogan

When I first came to CalArts I was a 26-year-old graduate student who had just moved from my parents' house in New Jersey after a fruitless three-year stab at making a name for myself in Brooklyn art-rock bands. I understood CalArts to be an important and good school. There were artists I respected a lot who attended and taught there. Painters and graphic designers who would not deem to sneeze at me with my BFA from the Maryland Institute College of Art suddenly held my gaze for entire moments once they heard I was going to CalArts. They said things like "you're going to the school with a pool." As exciting as that was, the most important thing about CalArts was that they were the only MFA program that accepted my application. Under no circumstances did I expect I'd end up spending 16 years patrolling its hallways trying to think of creative ways to ask nineteen-year-old performance artists to stop smoking weed indoors, but life is like that.

Don't Hate the Middle Management.

Hate the Game.

I got the job of Studio Manager immediately after graduating, and it was a difficult transition. The Studio Manager for the School of Art has a master key to hundreds of art studios, and is charged with ensuring that the students inside don't hurt themselves or burn the building down. One year I was getting drunk and smashing things in the studios, and the next I was telling people to stop getting drunk and smashing things in the studios. CalArts is known for being a freewheeling, anything-goes place, and I did not work in Theater, Film, Dance or Critical Studies, all of which still hewed to some traditional ideas of craft and self-discipline. In the School of Art, such notions were flouted, if not held in outright contempt. As a result, it was occasionally capable of transcendent beauty and innovation, but always a chaotic and exhausting thing to manage.

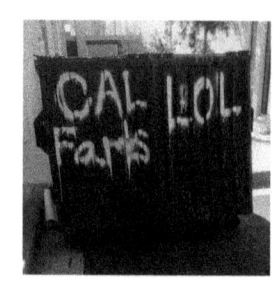

My job was to be one of maybe two or three people inside the Art School with the authority to say "no" to students, and I had to say no about the following things: No sleeping in the studio, no subletting the studio, no vandalizing the studio blocks, no smoking in the studio, no leaving your drug paraphernalia out and in clear view in your studio, no breaking Exit signs, no pulling fire alarms, no building lofts in your studio (fire marshall stuff), no couches that do not comply with California State Bulletin 117 in your studio (early years), no couches whatsoever in your studio (later years), no parties in your studio, no band practice in your studio, no converting your studio into a live music venue or dance club, no dogs left alone to howl forlornly for hours in your studio, no sleeping relatives, friends, or lovers in your studio, no full-size fridges in your studio, no constructing security systems for your studio involving pulley systems or shards of glass glued to blocks of wood, no mattresses in your studio, no hot plates in your studio, no blowtorches, no loose rats, snakes, chickens, or rabbits in your studio, no raising chickens or slaughtering chickens in studio areas, no running a "fight club" in your studio, no harboring local teenagers or eccentrics in your studio. It was a lot to deal with, and my power was largely symbolic.

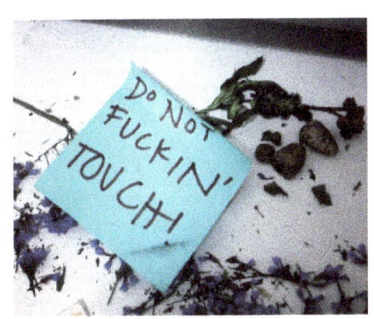

The flyers served as the watchful eyes of Big Brother, establishing the idea of my presence in corners where I was rarely actually present. I was one person, who had between 0-2 student workers at my disposal for a handful of hours on any given day. I had 172 studios I managed, serving 300 students, distributed across 5 campus buildings, and I also managed seven student galleries.

The tone of the flyers was important, and a tricky thing to nail. Given the scale of the people and places under my purview, I could not have students hating my guts. As someone who self identifies as "Artist," I did not want to be despised by my future cohort, and tactically, earning the enmity of students was counterproductive. There are no security cameras at CalArts, and the students do not snitch. If they hated me, all they would have to do is blow out a fire extinguisher in a studio block here, light a couch on fire there, kick some holes in the walls of a gallery and they'd have made my life significantly more difficult with no personal consequences. I am not an intimidating person by any reasonable standard, so bluffing with tough talk would have been unsuccessful. Eventually, I settled on the more authentic persona of Put-Upon-Moody-Neurotic, who many decide to cooperate with simply to spare the embarrassment and frustration of increasingly fraught studio checks and enforcement measures. Flyers were a way to telegraph all this — at their best they are funny, yet they contain a latent threat. While the theft or destruction of these flyers is not encouraged, it is expected, and certainly preferable to direct confrontation. They are available to be admired, defaced or despised at one's leisure, so long as their creator is kept out of it.

In the mid-2000s, CalArts was still operating in an alarmingly analogue fashion. Inter-office mail was delivered via reusable envelopes dating back decades. Work orders were filed using carbon paper. There was a large bulletin board in the art office, originally a muted light green, eventually painted a screaming loud red-orange, where memos were left for students under the first letter of their last name. This bulletin board was actually visited, these memos actually retrieved and read. Emails, on the other hand, were completely ignored. If you had something to tell someone and you emailed them, you may as well have written your message on a post-it note and thrown it in the trash. Phone calls and even a printed memo in their student mailbox were a better bet. For a school with a reputation for being on the cutting edge, its bureaucracy was entrenched in the expired twentieth century.

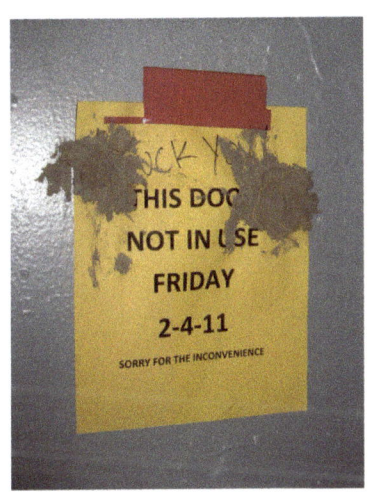

All that is to say, flyers were actually important. The hallways were covered in them and people would read them. You'd need to put up a ton of them because a lot of them would get stolen — and they needed to compete with the hundreds of other flyers people put up requesting voice over actors for animated short films, dancers/models for vague independent "projects," and someone to take the extra room in the local Valencia 3 Bedroom some grad students were renting.

Unlike many aspects of my job, they were something I understood and could actually control. I could not truly control undergrads' habitual flipping of Exit signs upside down, but I understood how to make a flyer that might make it seem like a dumb thing to do to other undergrads. I knew this audience. I had years of experience making posters for my band, coaxing my hipster comrades to one bar or another with nonsensical combinations of band names and weird images. CalArts undergraduates are practically the national template for hipsters, and their grad student counterparts were either aged or aspiring ones.

Finally, they served as a kind of therapy for me. A release valve for tension... I worked through the farcical nature of my position in public, to indicate to the students that I was aware enough to realize this was all absurd and they had no regard for it, but I would actually go through with it anyway. This mix of gallows humor and Authoritarian Lite came to define my herding approach for these feral cats we called art students.

Things have changed a lot since I started working at CalArts. There is a new President now. People read emails. Important faculty have passed on, or left for other opportunities, and new people have come in, guiding the school in new directions. As I'm writing this, Covid-19 has shut down the campus to student use for the better part of a year.

Until we get out from under the pandemic, CalArts is holding classes online. It is currently a school without a pool. Without students on campus, it is an easier place to tidy up and run in an orderly fashion, but of course the sense of futility in having things repaired only to have them destroyed again has been replaced with that of setting up a really nice work space for the use of nobody. While veteran faculty members might be beating their heads against their kitchen tables trying to teach conceptually-informed painting practice over their phones, I have been standing in empty rooms, screaming at the newly painted white walls on which I've just splattered gray floor paint. I wonder how it came to pass that Samuel Beckett wrote my job description. But in the back of my mind, I know the students will be back, bringing the life-force of the school with them. Should the students return, there will be even more risk — not just of fire, but of illness and even death. Even more new and unenforceable rules, and I'll have the privilege of saying "No" to a whole new list of art school transgressions.

DEAR JOHN,
Molly Jo Shea

If absolute power corrupts absolutely, does absolute powerlessness make you pure?
—Harry Shearer

It is tough being a man in America today. I don't mean a man's man, or a cis man, but a "man," man... like "The Man." It used to be that power was enough for respect. Now the rules are different. Maybe there is something to be said about technology shifting how we attract "clout," or maybe marketing has trained us to be skeptical of the same song and dance. Regardless, absolute power does not seem to be enough. You need to be in power, but look like you aren't. Now everyone wants to be liked. No one can be a decent villain these days. I miss the days of Damien Hirst making death sculptures. I miss the days of commercials telling me to just buy their stuff, not trying to be my friend. Why is my mayor claiming to support victims of racist police brutality while bending a knee, when he is unable to do something as simple as reallocating money out of the pockets of murderers and into funding social services — or heck — even helping with, I don't know — PLAGUE 2.0?

I find myself masked inside my car, driving up the 405, listening to KEarth 101, the saccharine-voiced DJs tell me to stand-up against racial injustice by filling out the US Census. Time to take a stand! ... by being counted. Who doesn't like being registered? You see, it's for our own benefit. Time to listen to the government pretending to be on our side, liquid sunshine poured into our ears from our sweet overlords, Love and Radio.

Next up, The Corrs, *Breathless*.

So go on, go on, come on
leave me breathless

Tempt me, tease me, until I can't deny
This loving feeling (loving feeling)
Make me long for your kiss
Go on (go on), go on (go on)
Yeah...

<u>Please don't spit in my face and tell me it's raining.</u>

How does one become a villain and still be loved? You get a middleman. In the breakdown of command from A to B, the middleman is the "to." The middleman is the connector, the arrow that points. Being CalArt's studio manager, John Hogan is that arrow. Always pointing, always directing, always begging you to open your eyes and recognize your reality. But an arrow isn't a letter, it isn't a noun, it is a verb. An arrow is a symbol of direction. CalArts wants something implemented, John is the voice box of the institution. In taking that role, John has had to keep students from destroying one of the school's greatest assets, their hallowed cocoons of creation and discovery — their studios. He makes sure students don't kill each other or fall asleep while making candle wax sculptures and emblaze the oil-bomb eucalyptus trees surrounding the campus. He has dealt with his own personal Slab City installations by the dumpsters near the Broad studios. Slab City installations that really really want to be Noah Purifoys. He has had to communicate with "cool people." He communicates with the depressed, the jaded, the over-eager, naïve, self-indulged children. How do you get someone to care when their whole *modus operandi* is not caring?

What happens when you know you are an arrow? What happens when the arrow becomes self-aware? What happens when you are pointed at a vulnerable group and don't really want to issue those commands? What happens when your navel starts to glow, and all you can do is follow your nose to regard it and its many depths?

Then the arrow makes a bend back towards power. It curls away from enacting and looks like a sad basset hound back to its owner. But the power feeds the arrow. The power created the arrow, and without it — the arrow might not exist at all. So, what can an arrow do? It keeps turning, it bends into itself. It becomes this symbol.

The replay, the u-turn, the symbol of self-deprecation. In ancient times it was known as the Ouroboros; the snake that eats its own tail. John Hogan's posters say "Go Fuck Yourself," but they also say, "Criminy — Fuck Me too, while we're at it." And when no one hears him, all he is able to do is repeat himself. John, our own personal town crier, sings his song again. Cursed to sing the same song over again, hoping someone will remember the chorus.

What I love about John's posters is that they use the system to comment on how down the system is, by making fun of all the parts of the larger story. What does it mean for a man who used to be a wacky performance art student at CalArts to chase down rich students to clean up after themselves, when they've had maids to clean up after themselves their entire lives, in order to enable a new crop of dirtbag students to come and spend fucktons of money to sustain a flailing institution that keeps ideologies of non-materiality and non-craft afloat by simple repetition, so it does not need to finally fix those facilities that were trashed by the jaded Little Lord Fauntleroys that came beforehand?

Maybe CalArts is not as glamorous as the Ouroboros. It actually takes a lot of effort to suck your own dick (so I am told). CalArts, after all, is all about community. It is about working together to repeat ourselves over and over again.

Such is the Sisyphean curse of an artistic practice. Recycling the same artwork from the 60s, 70s, 80s, 90s — ugh — and now the aughts! After all... You oughta know.

> *And I'm here, to remind you*
> *Of the mess you left when you went away.*
> *It's not fair, to deny me*
> *Of the cross I bear that you gave to me.*
> *You, you, you oughta know.*
> —Alanis Morrissette.

So maybe the system is more like...

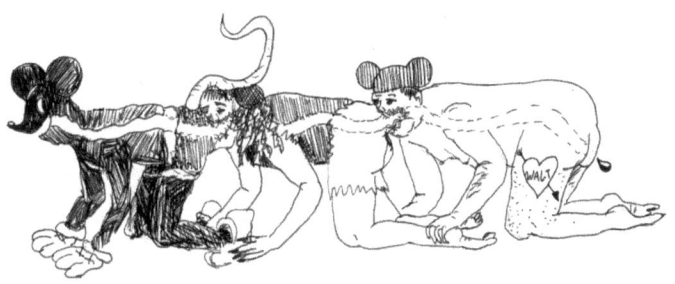

Poor John is in the worst spot of this human centipede. Poor John is the middleman and he does so much to warn us what's coming down the pipeline. And what do we students do? We bite him in the ass.

What those of us at the end of the human centipede do not realize is that one day someone new will sew someone into *our* butthole and we'll be shoveling shit down someone else's throat. How do I know? Because I used to be an administrator at an art school too.

The only way I did it for three years was by making softcore, nail erotica during my lunch break. Slowly piercing twinkies with my overly manicured hands while I decompressed from spiraling conversations with helicopter parents. I saw students forced to leave campus on their first day of school because their parents didn't pay tuition. I have had to tell students even though their portfolios were flawless, that they didn't have enough money or student loans to enter the pearly gates of accepted weirdodom. I have sat quietly while I watched 16-year-olds sob in my cubical because their parents didn't understand the only thing that provided solace during the hell that is puberty was the freedom found in creativity and art. Now they were being urged to abandon those freedoms.

So. It is now time to say sorry to John. Whatever it was you did that you know was wrong, or you overreacted to in the heat of the moment, you need to atone for it. We need to apologize because people will always be added to the front of the poop chain, and we'll always have people added to the end of the chain. Absolve your Art Trash Sins and realize that Karma is a bitch, and I'm not talking about that freegan dying her pubes green and making bongs in ceramics; she's actually pretty chill. OK. I'll start.

Dear John,

I'm sorry that I gave myself a UTI from peeing in a giant Squirt™ bottle in my studio because I didn't want to get caught sneaking to the bathroom at 1 a.m. because I was pulling an all nighter in my studio and didn't want the ancient CalArts fuzz to catch me snoozin'. I'm also sorry if I ended up growing mold in there a couple of times. I'm also sorry / not sorry for gettin' some action in the studios. But overall, I loved my studio at CalArts and tried to treat the space with respect and love knowing someone else would be following in my footsteps.

Here are some more apologies:
Forgive me overloard, for I have sinned. I regularly sleep in my studio and have a "plinth" that acts as a cover over my folding mattress.

I have an almost year old jar of my own pee that has been sitting on top of my mini fridge since last september. I've also had sex in there like 5 or 6 times.

I lived in my studio pretty much all of my second year.

I'd burn candles in my studio and when John saw a candle on my trunk/desk and said, "make sure you don't light those in here!" I said, "Oh god! I'd never! I have them here for a project I'm working on. They won't be lit."

I had a cot and a hammock that was bolted to the walls... that I may or may not have used to live there haha!

...

Thank you, John, for making us laugh as we repeat ourselves. Thank you for never telling us that we are just an echo. I've had to watch you eat your own tail many-a-time when delivering the next meal down the pipeline. That's why your Karaoke swan song should be heard at every CalArts Christmas party. As a reminder to not pick a fight with the person whose butt is sewn into your face, but to the weird German guy who did it in the first place.

> *Sailors fighting in the dance hall*
> *Oh man, look at those cavemen go*
> *It's the freakiest show*
> *Take a look at the lawman*
> *Beating up the wrong guy*
> *Oh man, wonder if he'll ever know*
> *He's in the best selling show*
> *Is there life on Mars?*

—David Bowie (as sung by John P. Hogan)

As part of this book, I think it is
appropriate that we have a section
available for your own apology to John
Hogan, right here.

Dear John,

Yours!

THE BALLAD OF THE RELUCTANT INSTITUTIONALIST

Michael Ned Holte

A few years before I knew him as the Studio and Gallery Manager for the CalArts School of Art, I first encountered John P. Hogan as the triumphal vocalist for the colonialist art band Ponce de Leon. It was late 2005, on a temporary stage plunked down in the parking lot of the new grad studio building at USC, where I worked at the time. Ponce de Leon was opening for The Bushes, an artist rap duo that wore matching green turtlenecks and sweatpants — the latter name referred to foliage, not the then-current occupants of the White House — and was on the bill because one of the group's dancers and singers (a.k.a. "the party-back") was in the MFA program at USC. Needless to say, Ponce de Leon took its name from the Spanish explorer who hopelessly sought the mythical fountain of youth and trampled much of indigenous Florida in the process.

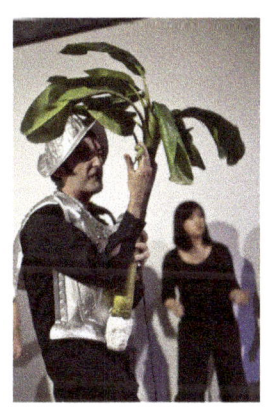

The band's gambit was explicitly conceptual and admittedly absurd. In fact, it resembled thrifty musical theater — I'm thinking about Jill Kroesen's *Excuse Me I Feel Like Multiplying* (1980), for example — as much as anything. According to the band's self-analysis, "Ponce de Leon seeks to reconcile the sexualized hipster death drive with the liberal establishment's need for order. PDL intended to allow for the underground art/music scenester to face his/her imperialist impulse directly. Ponce De Leon was conceived with the idea that, if we have a collective need or will to impose our belief system on others, we should at least acknowledge, accept, and confront it without guilt or insincere self-reproach." It should also be said that the songs, co-written with Gregory McKenna, were abundantly catchy. I am embarrassed to admit how long their lament, "I Sing My Regrets to the Egrets," continued to linger in my head.

John went to grad school in the CalArts Program in Art and later joined its staff. Once I came to teach in that program in 2009, I got to know John as a colleague and more clearly recognized the (post-)colonial impulses behind Ponce de Leon's zealous mission. PDL had emerged from a context in which "criticality" was anticipated and implied in every gesture, big or small. In this sense, nothing CalArts art students do is "extracurricular" — even the punk bands that play long after most faculty leave for the day assume Marxian analysis at the very least. In 2009, I had another chance to see PDL perform at Machine Project, the eclectic non-profit founded by Mark Allen, another graduate of the CalArts art program. Machine Project, under Allen's guidance, managed to merge the inherited tactics of a more studious institutional critique with a penchant for manic performativity — one that frequently consorted with the common (meaning popular and also debased) culture.

Mike Kelley, who graduated from CalArts in the late 1970s, is an obvious precedent for this dialectical synthesis — John has cited him as an influence and siren song that brought him to Los Angeles and CalArts. I can relate: Mike was one of my teachers at Art Center, where I went to grad school, and like John I first became aware of him because of his cover art for Sonic Youth's 1992 album *Dirty*. A number of Mike's significant works situate CalArts not only as an institution, but as *The Institution*, and in so doing stress test its highfalutin critical rhetoric by subjecting it to the abject potential of the school's subterranean debauchery, most obviously emblematized by its Sublevel — literally, a subterranean level "zero" that is ridden with juvenile graffiti sanctioned by the institute.

Mike's installation *From My Institution to Yours* (1987) was made while he was a visiting member of the faculty at CalArts, on a part of the mezzanine that is now a suite of small studios for photo students. And his *Pay For Your Pleasure* (1988), in which a hallway of banners of artists and philosophers extolling the virtues of criminality led viewers to a painting by an actual serial killer and a donation box, always struck me as an acidic, hyperbolic riposte to what he likely perceived as the pieties of artists like Hans Haacke and Michael Asher. The former's *MoMA Poll* (1970) was a politically loaded installation that invited the direct participation of visitors to that museum; the latter's Post-Studio Critique class, notorious for its remarkably lengthy sessions, holds enormous influence in the CalArts art school pedagogy and its mythology.

Asher was a figure of (almost) unquestioned authority in an institution that is habitually suspicious of authority. So, I eventually came to understand Mike's "institutional" works as a kind of Oedipal reaction to Asher as the pedagogical father, even as they also inevitably revealed his influence. Circa 1990, Mike initiated a series of felt banners, influenced by Sister Corita Kent, that replicated flyers found on college bulletin boards. These include a call for an actor to play Pier Paolo Pasolini ("knowledge of italian an asset") and a poster for a lecture by attorney Chokwe Lumumba, sponsored by the African Student Union. One flyer seemingly requested nothing more than a reader's attention, declaring:

> PANTS
> SHITTER
> &
> PROUD
> P.S.
> JERK-
> OFF
> TOO
>
> (AND I WEAR GLASSES)

Belatedly — now — I wonder how many of these flyers were initially found at CalArts: some, perhaps most, possibly all of them? One of the most incredible features of the strange and disorienting main building of CalArts is its vast network of bulletin boards that accumulate a dense thicket of flyers over the course of a semester. In totality, these flyers represent the cooperative, unregulated discourse of the institution far better than any well-intended, top-down approach could ever hope to. (I am writing this in the midst of a pandemic, preparing to begin the new academic year teaching through a corporate web portal, aware that the bulletin boards will likely remain depressingly empty for a long time.) Often these flyers are highly pragmatic and informative, but just as often they are befuddling, outlandish, or illegible. Sometimes they are all of the above, especially in proximity to one another. Readers are often left to decide.

In his guise as Studio and Gallery Manager for the CalArts School of Art, John is responsible for some of the flyers that become part of this institutional communication network. They are official business, made on company time, but they often carefully camouflage their authority. While primarily directed at the art students that remain under his weary watch, and most often appearing in close proximity to the School of Art office, its classrooms, and its studios, John's flyers are inevitably absorbed into the larger welter of collective expression. Viewed in isolation, as an ongoing body of work, his flyers prove to be reliably informative, with a consistent, not-so-hidden message: "You'd be dumb to not pay attention to this." But to get the attention of art students — a spectrum of free thinkers and troublemakers, generally speaking — one needs to speak the lingua franca of the art school, which is to say the flyers need to *be* art, or at least operate in the vicinity of it, willingly offering themselves up for critical scrutiny, even as they need to wield a voice of authority. John is unfailingly polite, in my experience, but he is also an artist who doesn't suffer fools or at least foolishness without a certain amount of palpable agony. And I've suffered with him at times, particularly in my years as a co-director of the art program. These flyers evince the agony of the unlikely authority figure; they are the ballads of a reluctant institutionalist.

It's hard to pick favorites among this collection, but one of mine features Henry Rollins, the bellicose singer for Black Flag who evolved into an avuncular voice of authority about all things cool and *indy*. (If your skin is crawling, you get the idea.) The picture of vintage Rollins with arms crossed, muscles bulging, immediately growls, "Don't fuck with me."

And if I have the semiotics right, it might even go a step farther and say, "I'd kick your ass if I didn't have this enviable wall of vintage jazz records to listen to instead." John matches Hank's no-nonsense intensity with an equally no-nonsense sans serif, all-caps font that reads:

> MFA-2's:
> YOU MUST MOVE IN TO YOUR NEW STUDIO BEFORE MONDAY, 9/20
>
> DON'T THINK ABOUT IT...

Then, below the picture of Rollins, in an even bigger point size, he concludes:

> DO IT.

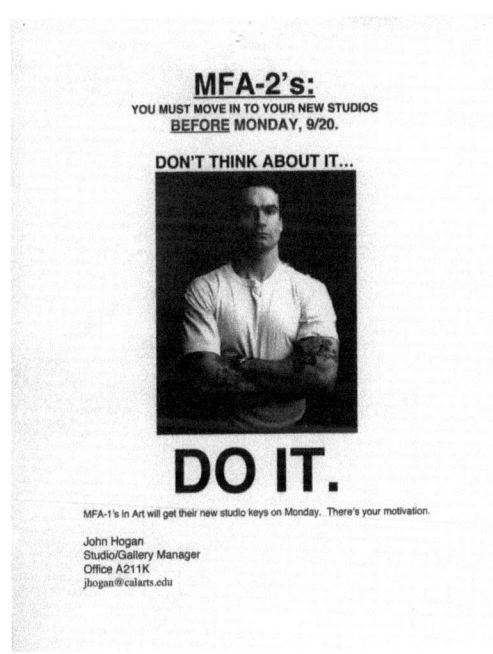

And below that he gently notes that, "MFA-1's in Art will get their new studio keys on Monday. There's your motivation." Rollins was surely there to get your attention, but by the bottom of the flyer he proves to be something of a red herring. Then again he also serves as a funny stand-in for John, one that similarly has power — and knows it — but is also a little embarrassed by it. Like: "Don't be a dick, so I don't have to be a dick."

Most of the flyers carry this message, if you're paying attention. And usually John leaves abundant clues for how the message should be read, often telegraphing the subtext as well as his awareness of how the message could be (willfully) misread. In other words, Art Students, he's one of you and knows your game better than you do. And he wants you to know that, too. In the case of Rollins, credibility as a hardcore ass kicker was traded in for a bookish radio show on KCRW. In John's case, he's the key master for students wanting access to their studio — or at least the key broker. He wants to get you into your studio, so you can concentrate on making art, and in exchange you can leave him in peace — to get to his studio, too, to make some drawings or a new performance or another record. Like these flyers, it's a good trade-off.

John's flyers inhabit the dialectical tension previously identified in the manifesto of Ponce de Leon, "[seeking] to reconcile the sexualized hipster death drive with the liberal establishment's need for order." What becomes excruciatingly funny, of course, is how the hipster eventually, if not inevitably, becomes the establishment. Imposing or perpetuating an institutional belief system, even one that openly and regularly questions authoritarian structures or authoritative gestures, these flyers slyly "acknowledge, accept, and confront" their author's begrudgingly "imperial impulses." Whether they do so "without guilt or insincere self-reproach" remains a question — one that keeps these missives balanced on the precarious threshold between bureaucratic functionality and art. That they often teeter over to the latter side is surely a product of their context and the space they create for the viewer or reader to get implicated and ensnared, because, dear CalArtian, his institution is your institution, too.

STUDIO LOTTERIES

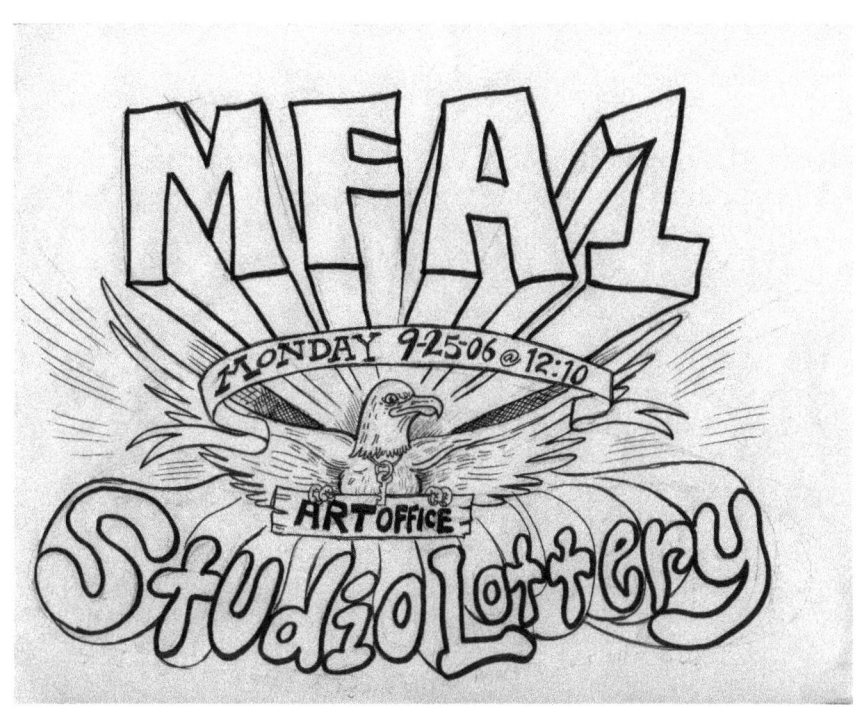

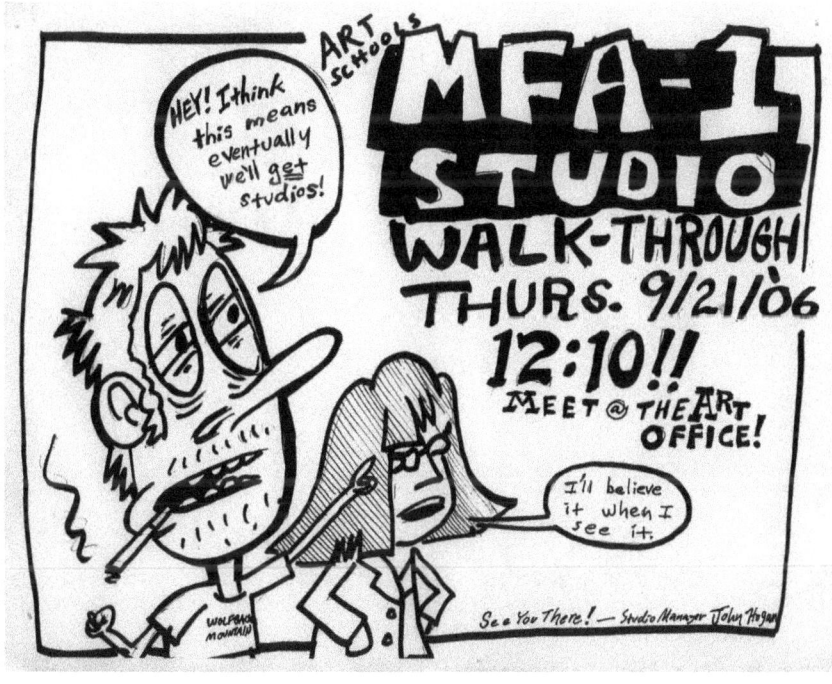

STUDIO LOTTERIES /

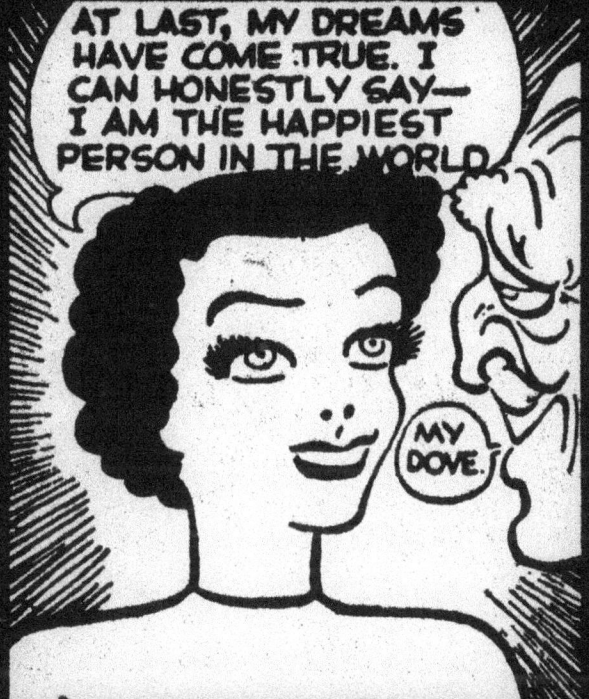

ATTENTION ART MFA-1s!!!!

THE LOTTERY

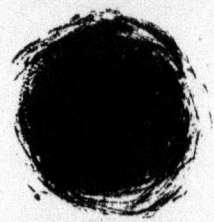

for MFA-2 Studios, Fall 2014*
is TUESDAY MAY 20th
at 12:00 PM!!
at the Annex/Broad Courtyard!
BE THERE!!!

*meaning the studios you will have next year when you're a MFA-2.

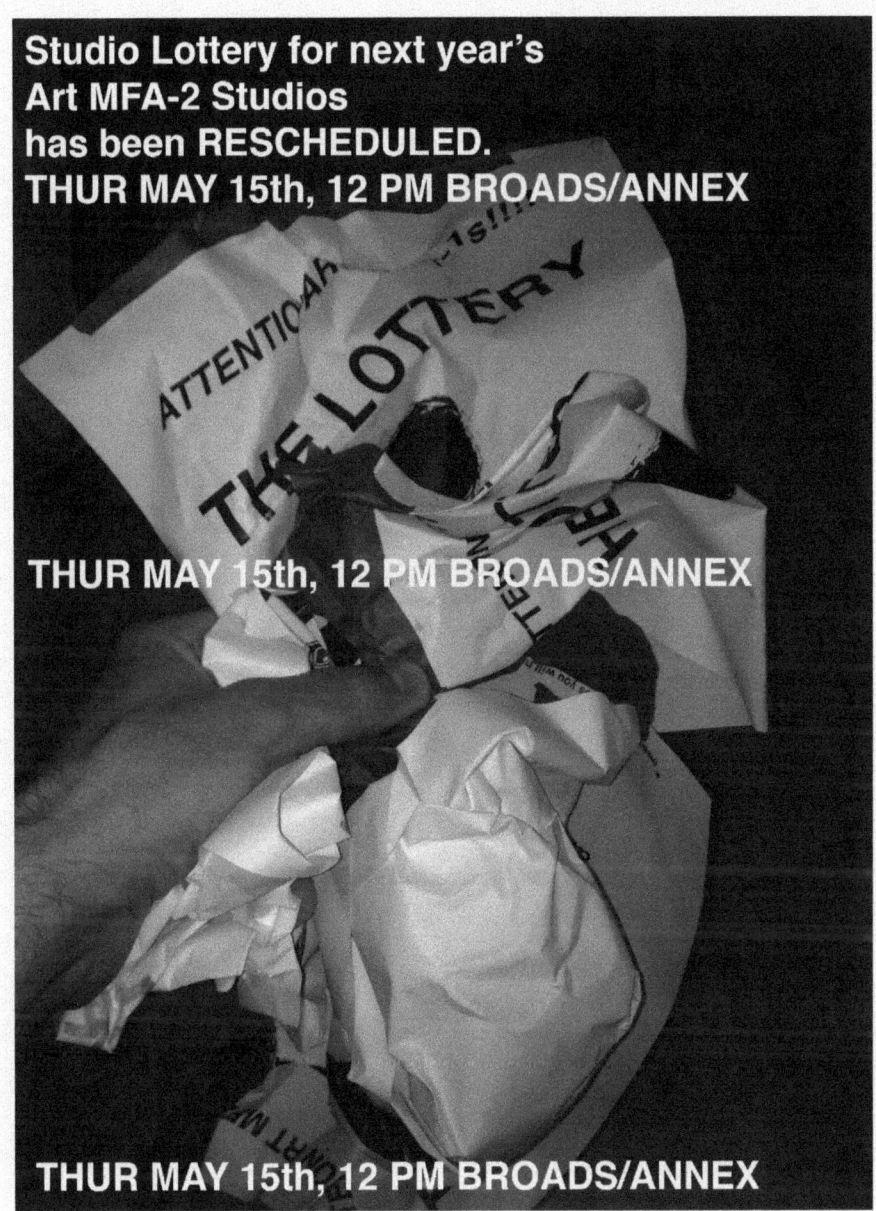

ATTENTION
ART PROGRAM MFA-1's

Don't Be Scared!!

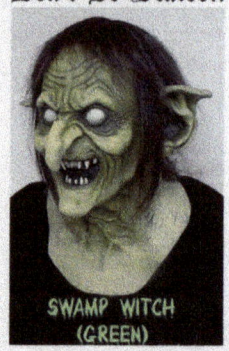

I Have something I need to Tell You!
Make a note of these Important Dates!!!!

MFA-1 STUDIO TOUR
THIS THURSDAY

Sep. 11th @ 12 noon. We start in the Art Office.

MFA-1 STUDIO LOTTERY

TUE. SEP. 16th @ 12 noon. in the Art Office.

Contact John Hogan with questions or problems:
jhogan@calarts.edu, Office A211K, (6610 222-2795

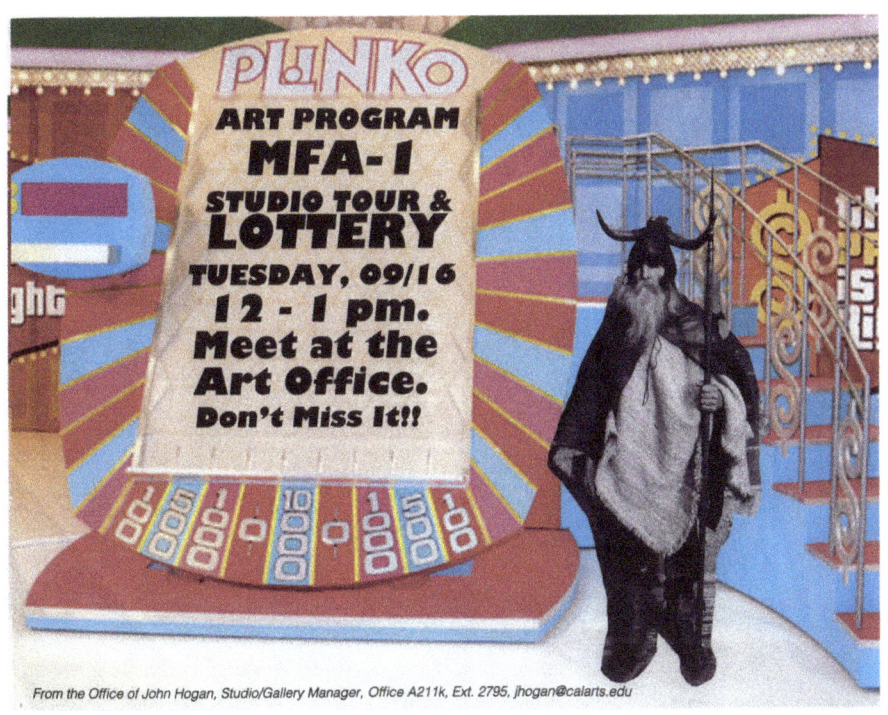

From the Office of John Hogan, Studio/Gallery Manager, Office A211k, Ext. 2795, jhogan@calarts.edu

ATTENTION PHOTO MFAs!!!

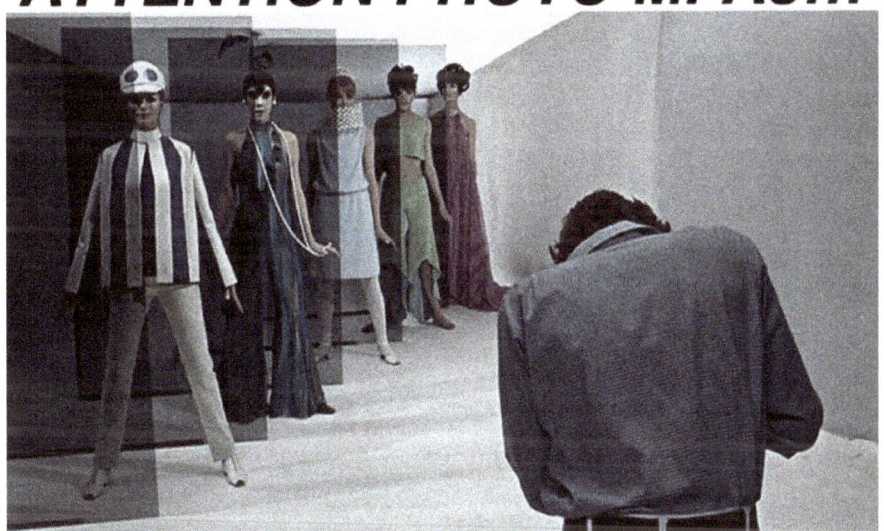

Photo/Media MFA-1 Studio Tour & Lottery
Wednesday, September 17th, 12 noon (Before Grad Crit)!!
Meet at the Art Office! This is important. Don't Miss It!!!

STUDIO LOTTERIES / 39

COWABUNGA, MFA-1s in ART!
IT'S A LOTTERY FOR FALL 2015 STUDIOS
where you find out what STUDIO you get when you're a MFA-2!!
Broads, Annexes, and others will be up for grabs. omg when!?

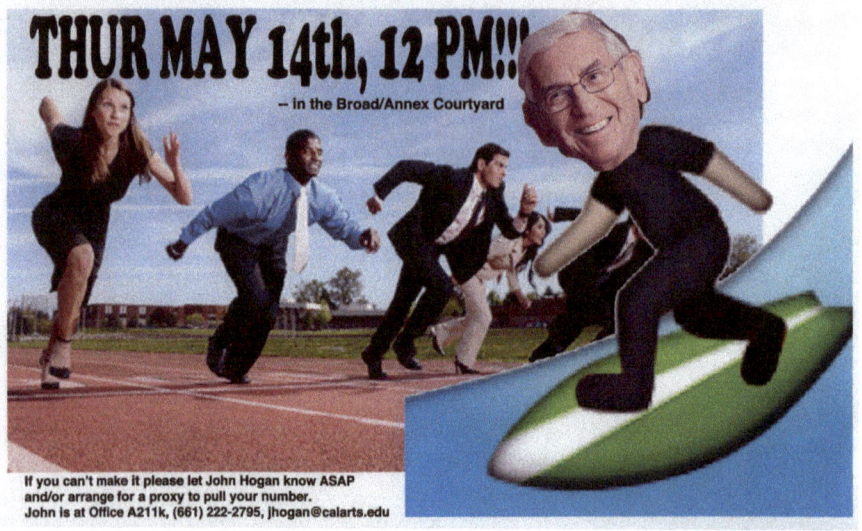

If you can't make it please let John Hogan know ASAP and/or arrange for a proxy to pull your number.
John is at Office A211k, (661) 222-2795, jhogan@calarts.edu

WAKE UP!!! THIS IS IMPORTANT!!!

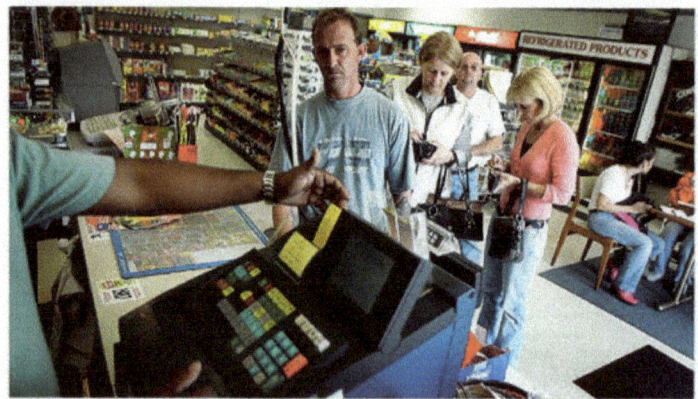

STUDIO LOTTERY for CURRENT ART MFA-1's!!
Will you get a Broad? An Annex? An A202?
Only your personal preferences and
Lady Luck can decide! DON'T MISS THIS!!
12 Noon! Thur. May 16th! Broad Courtyard!!

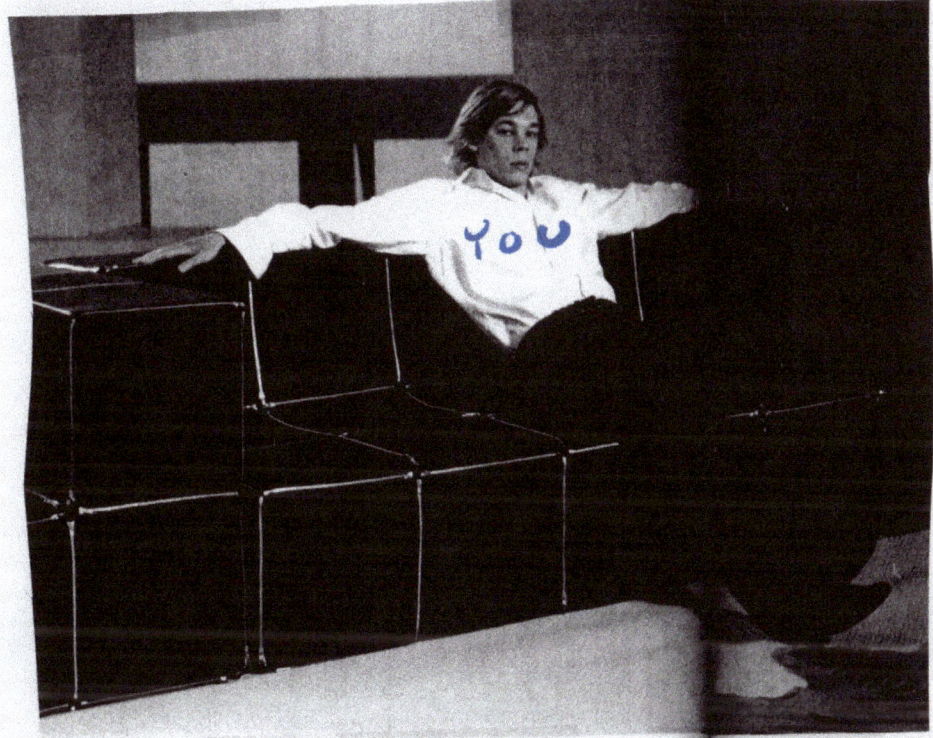

STUDIO LOTTERIES / 41

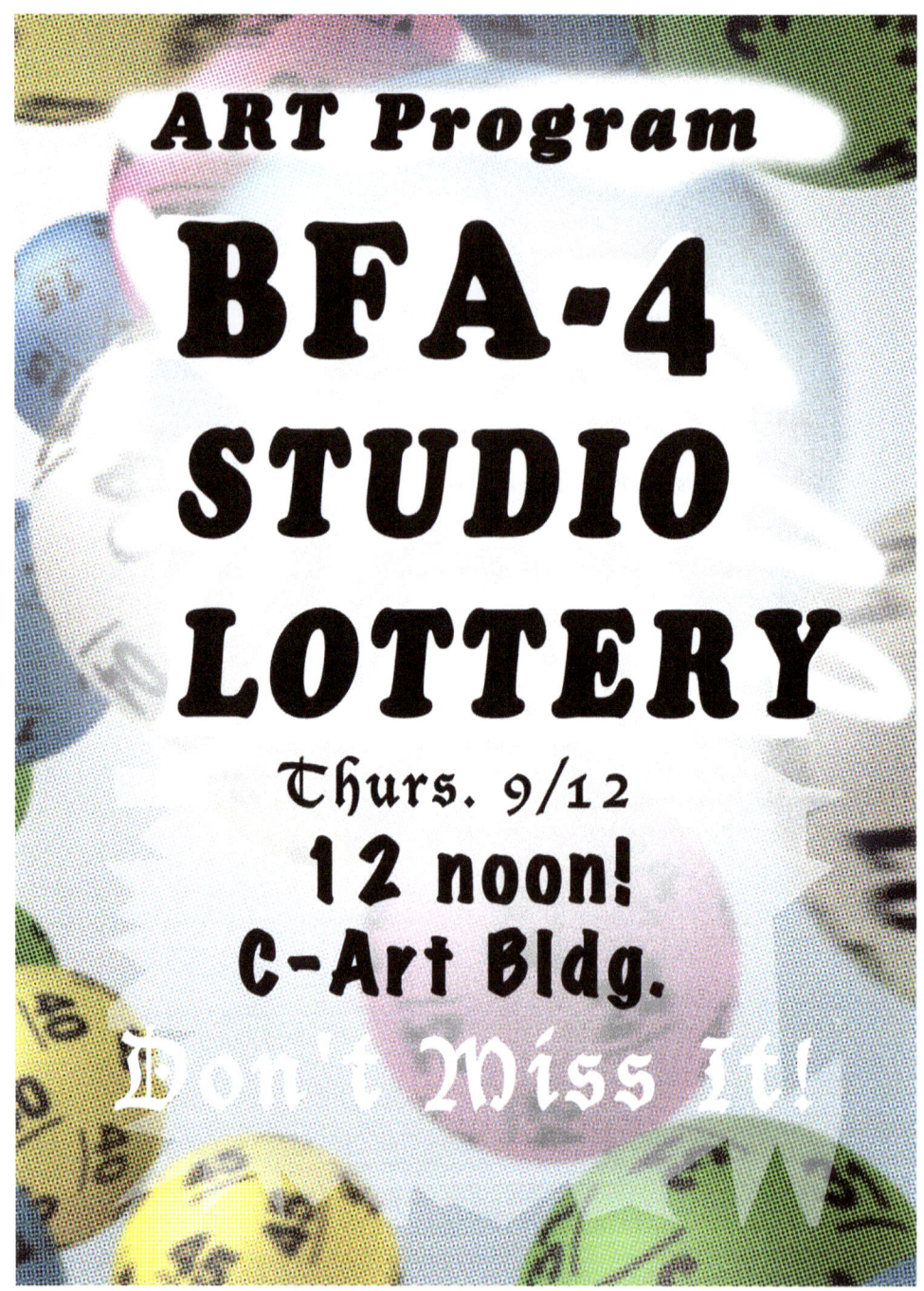

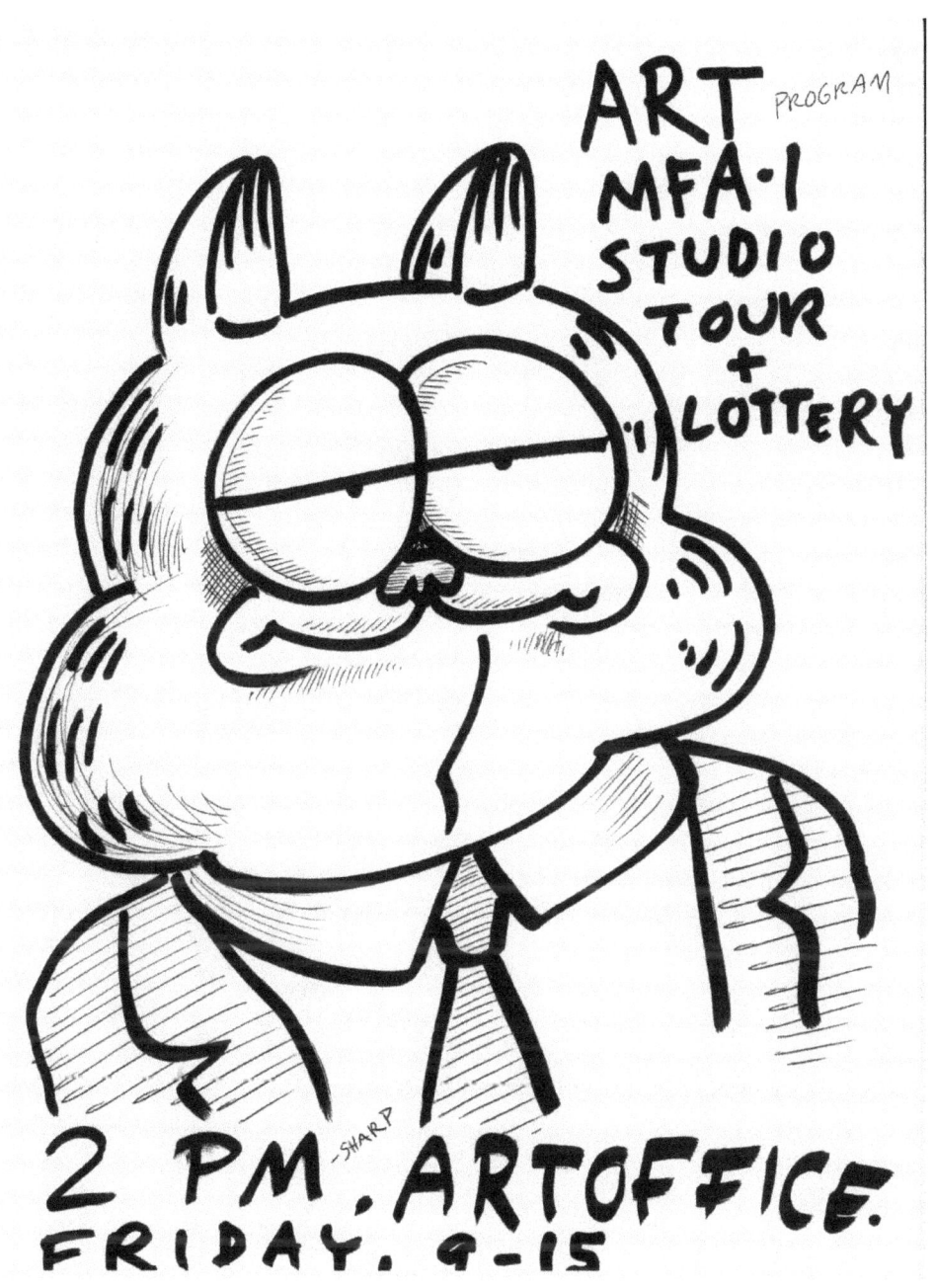

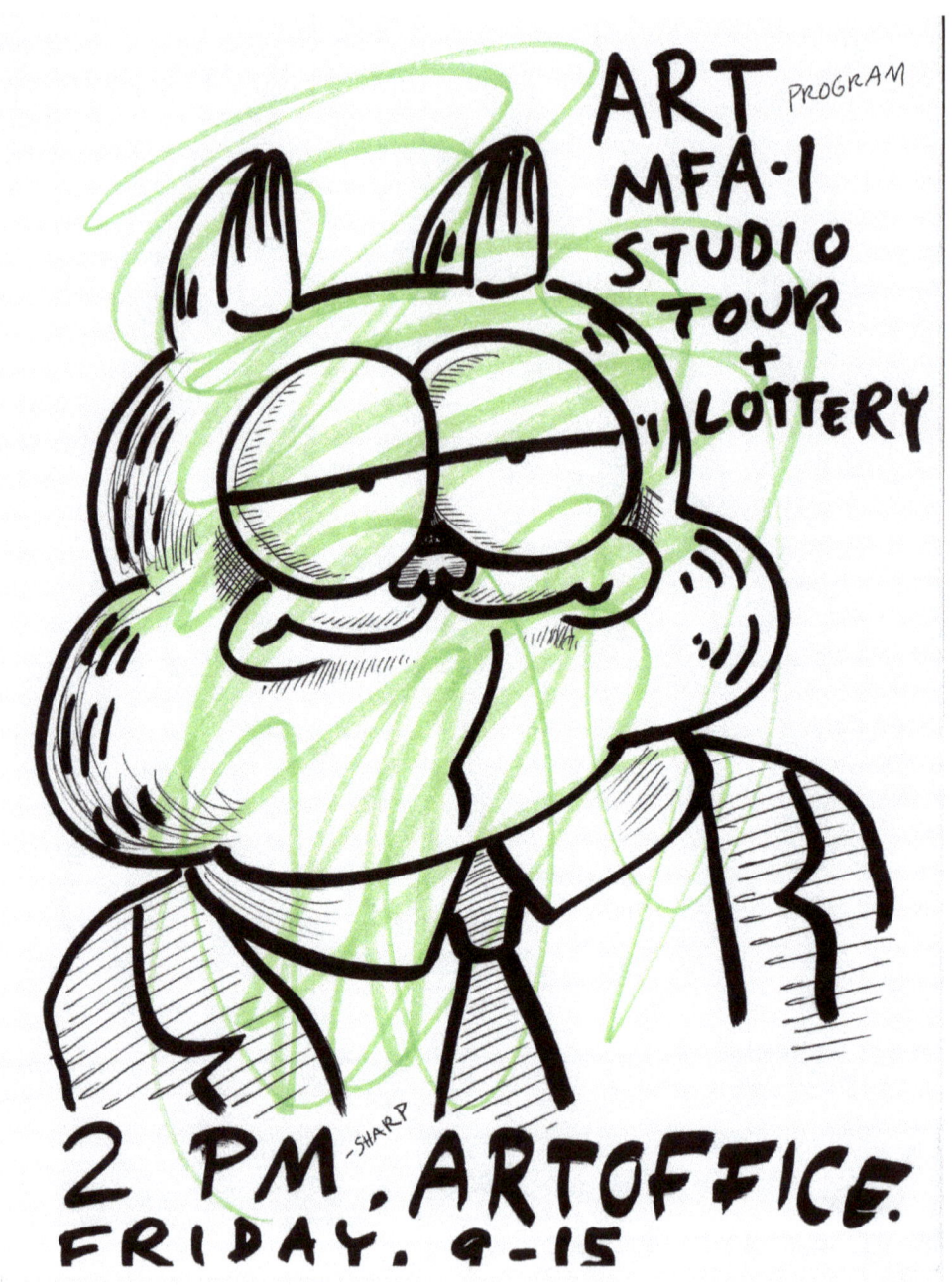

DAY-TO-DAY HECTORING

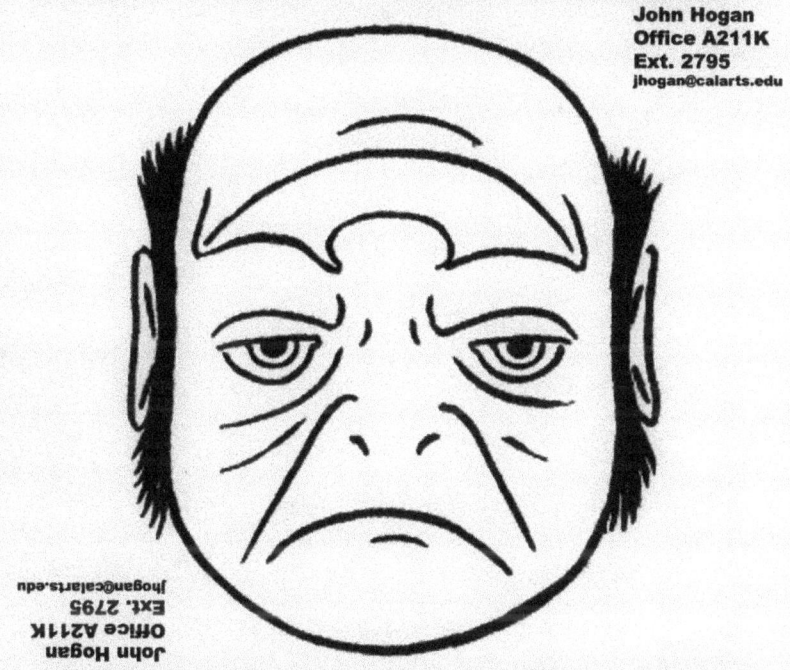

Drawing/Painting/Graffiti-ing on Fire Hazard Equipment is A Misdemeanor, So DON'T Do That Anymore.

-John Hogan, Studio Manager
Office A211K
661-222-2795

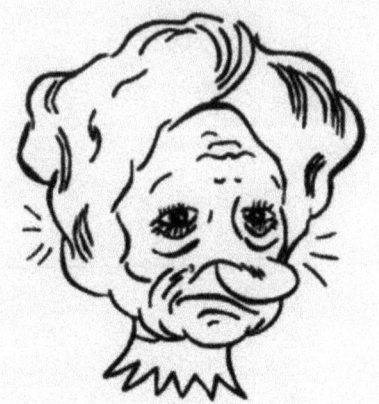

-John Hogan, Studio Manager
Office A211K
661-222-2795

Drawing/Painting/Graffiti-ing on Fire Hazard Equipment is A Misdemeanor, So DON'T Do That Anymore.

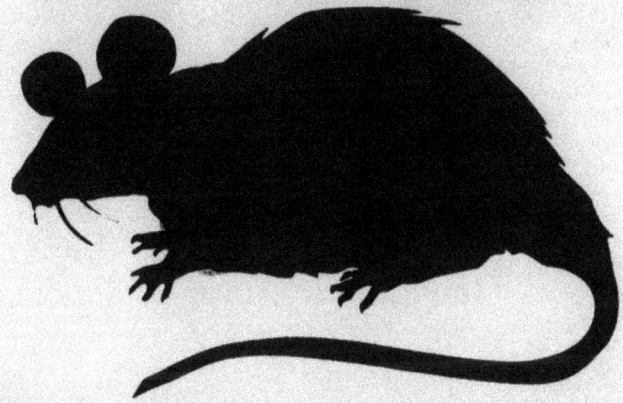

DO NOT FEED THE VERMIN.

Please put all food in a sealable, airtight container (you know, like Tupperware). This includes dog food and the like. And for goodness sakes, please **do NOT leave unfinished food sitting out on your desk/floor/etc.** There are these things called "mice" and these other things called "rats": They love that stuff and they totally will get in and eat it if you leave it out. They start out cute, but every once in a while they do something like **poop on your art** or **carry the plague**. We are working to eradicate such nastiness from the studios, but we still need your help. Thanks!!

John Hogan
Studio Manager
Ext. 2795
Office A211K
jhogan@calarts.edu

HEY EVERYBODY!
HERE'S A BACK-TO-SCHOOL REMINDER:
YOU'RE NOT SUPPOSED TO VANDALIZE THE SCHOOL.

IT IS EXTREMELY EXPENSIVE AND TIME-CONSUMING TO CONSTANTLY CLEAN UP ALL THIS GRAFFITI. IF YOU'D LIKE BETTER GALLERY LIGHTING, WORKING FACILITIES, AND A GENERALLY IMPROVED EXPERIENCE AT THE SCHOOL, PLEASE BEAR IN MIND THAT A GIGANTIC CHUNK OF THE GALLERY/STUDIO BUDGET WILL PROBABLY HAVE BEEN SPENT PAINTING OVER SMILEY FACES AND POWER-WASHING DRAWINGS OF BIRTHDAY CAKES AND CANABIS PLANTS OFF THE GROUND. I *WISH* I WERE JOKING!

DO NOT SPRAY-PAINT ON THE PAVEMENT OR THE WALLS OF THE BUILDING. VANDALIZING SCHOOL PROPERTY WILL RESULT IN FINES AND LOSS OF STUDIO PRIVELEGES.

MAKE SURE TO TELL YOUR FRIENDS, AND THANKS FOR THE COOPERATION!

JOHN HOGAN
STUDIO MANAGER
OFFICE A211K
(661) 222-2795
jhogan@calarts.edu

Beware, ye students!
The Halloween Party is upon us!!

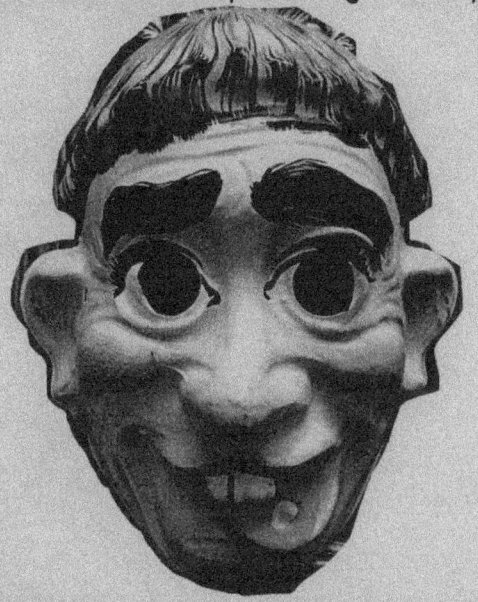

The Halloween Party is this Friday. There will be all manner of drunken, belligerent, Dionyssian behavior. Some people will be students, others will be alumni, and others might be **uninvited cretinous ghouls**. When I say uninvited cretinous ghouls I mean *"suspicious characters"*, not *"ghosts"*!

Please be careful, lock up your studio good, lock up your studio block good, hang out in groups, and please do not hesitate to call Security if you see anyone suspicious in your studio block or on campus in general.

Be Safe! Have fun! Don't Break Stuff!

Studio/Gallery Manager
Office A211K
jhogan@calarts.edu
(661) 222-2795

SECURITY = 661-222-2702

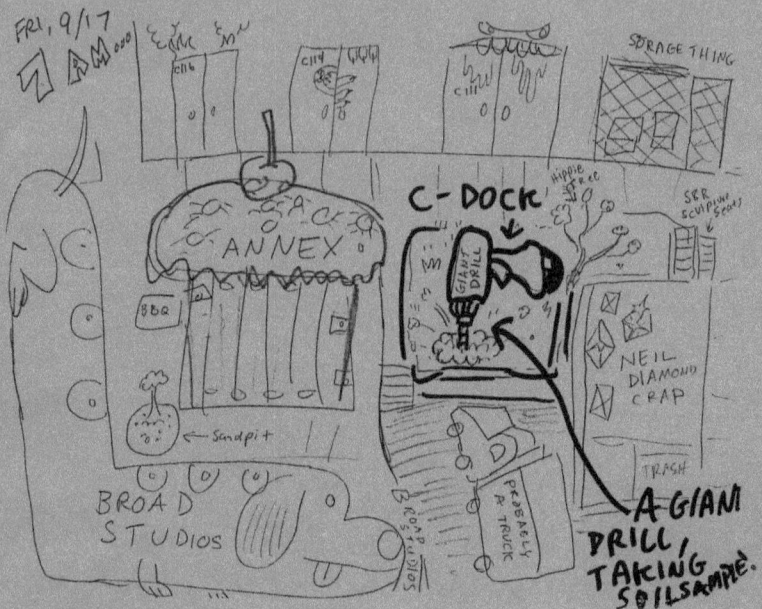

5/19/08

I WILL THROW YOUR **FRIENDSHIP CRAP*** FROM **FRIENDSHIP PARK** INTO THE **FRIENDSHIP DUMPSTER** ON WED. MAY 28th, UNLESS YOU HIDE IT FROM ME FIRST.

* — The word "CRAP" can refer to ART or TRASH.

———————————————

— JOHN HOGAN, Studio MGMT ©
       x2795, etc.

DAY-TO-DAY HECTORING / 53

ITEMS IN THIS AREA WILL BE
DISCARDED
03/03/20
or anytime thereafter.
PLEASE REMOVE IMMEDIATELY OR CONTACT STUDIO MANAGEMENT w/ QUESTIONS.

Studio Manager
Office A211K
(661) 222-2795
jhogan@calarts.edu

RAIN, WHAT?

PEOPLE OF THE BROAD/ANNEX WORLD,

It's going to rain, which is CRAZY.

People in the Broads, make sure you keep art off the floor, as the Broads sometimes flood. Am I suggesting you make your art float in the air? What are you supposed to do?? I don't know put it on a table or a shelf I'm sorry they make me put these fliers out, it sucks to have your art messed up by dumb water.

If you have any leaking in your studio, please contact the Facilities Office or me as soon as you can. If the leaks happen outside of regular operating hours, please contact Campus Safety/Security and they will address the issue as best they can.

JOHN HOGAN (Studio Manager):

(661) 222-2795, jhogan@calarts.edu

FACILITIES: (661) 253-7807

CAMPUS SAFETY: (661) 222-2702

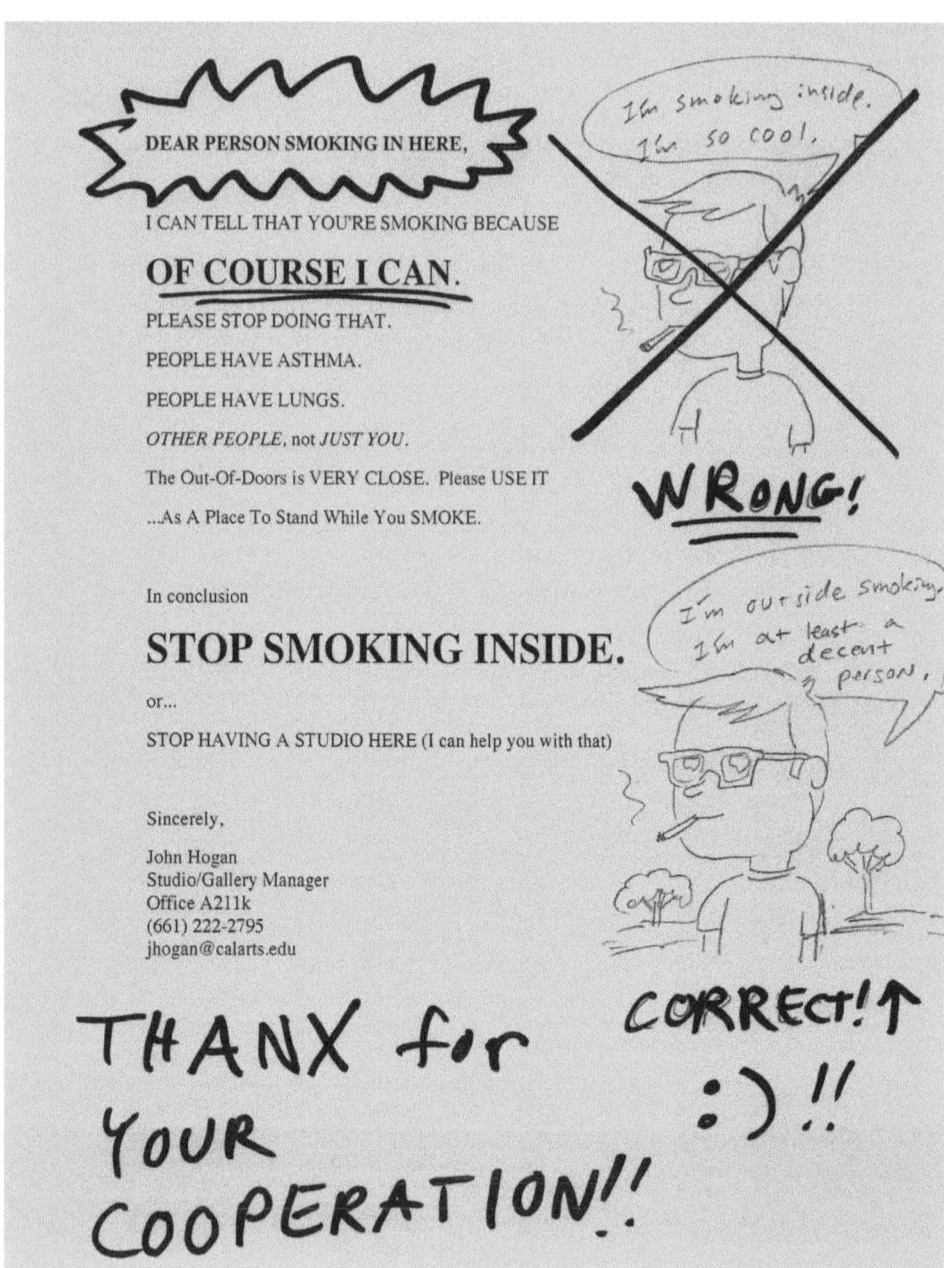

HEAR YE! HEAR YE!
THIS GROUNDED TREEHOUSE/SHANTYTOWN/SLAUGHTERLOG/ETC. STRUCTURE NEEDS TO BE "MADE OFFICIAL" IN ORDER TO SURVIVE.

WHAT DOES THAT MEAN??

It means someone needs to fill out paperwork with Facilities Management and have it approved, or else this structure will be dismantled and discarded entirely on

Mon. April 26th.

WHAAAAAAAAT....!!!???

Hold on, just wait a sec. The Art School will let you keep this thing up until May 17th, they just need a student or group of students to vouch for it. Isn't that great? They are nice.

Yeah, but I bet there's some stipulation that I will resent.

Well, it'll be subject to the same safety standards as the rest of the Institute, meaning that if you want to keep this thing standing, you can't smoke in it and you can't sleep in it, you can't perform surgery in it, you can't act as a midwife in it, you can't raise livestock in it, and the whole thing will still have to come down by May 17th.

So let's say I want it to stay because I love it and am ready to take responsibility for things.

Then just traipse up to John Hogan's office and tell him you want to fill out the paperwork and make this an Institute-approved artwork.

And let's say I don't care and want to wash my hands of this whole thing?

Then just do nothing and we'll throw it out on April 26th.

What if I am interested in being a helpful person?

Then you can help us clean this thing when we clean it up! We'll probably start around 1:30pm on the 26th if no one claims it.

What if I'm not an art student and I want to adopt this thing but I don't want to sign paperwork...

No.

Any more Questions, please contact
John Hogan, Office A211K jhogan@calarts.edu 661-222-2795

DO NOT LEAVE THE DOORS PROPPED OPEN.

DO NOT LEAVE THE DOORS PROPPED OPEN.

ALSO, DO NOT LEAVE THE DOORS PROPPED OPEN.

John Hogan
Studio/Gallery Manager
Office A211K
jhogan@calarts.edu
661-222-2795

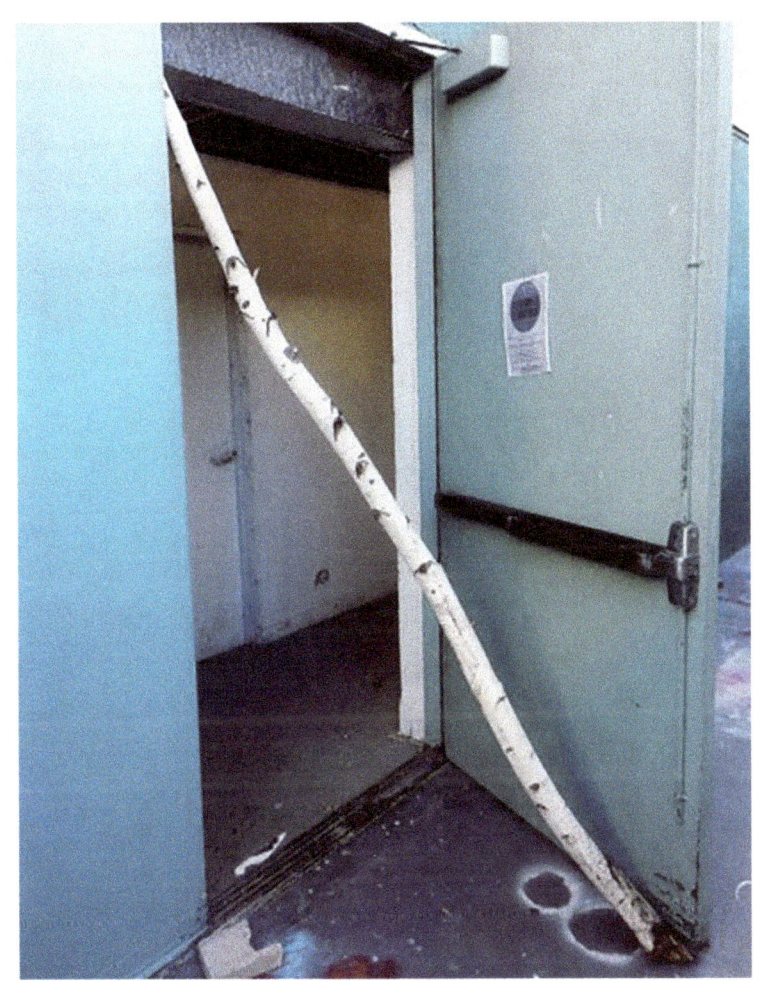

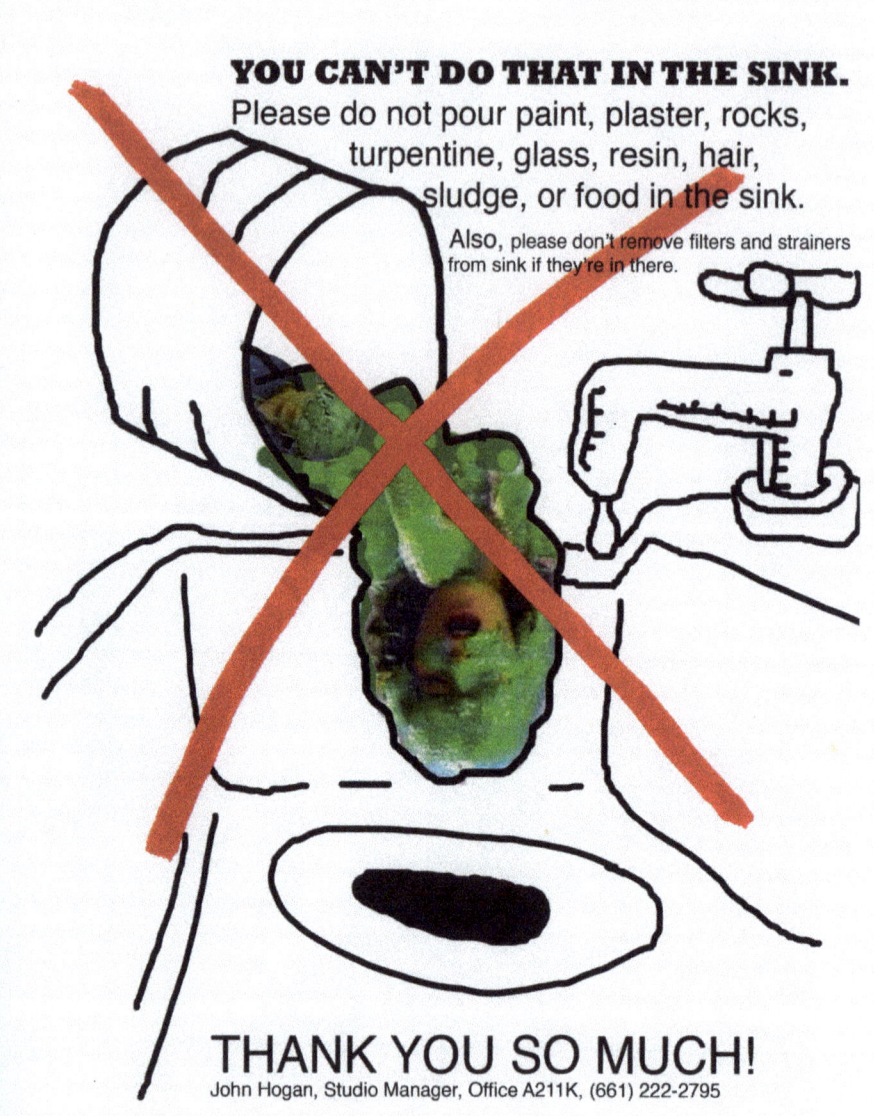

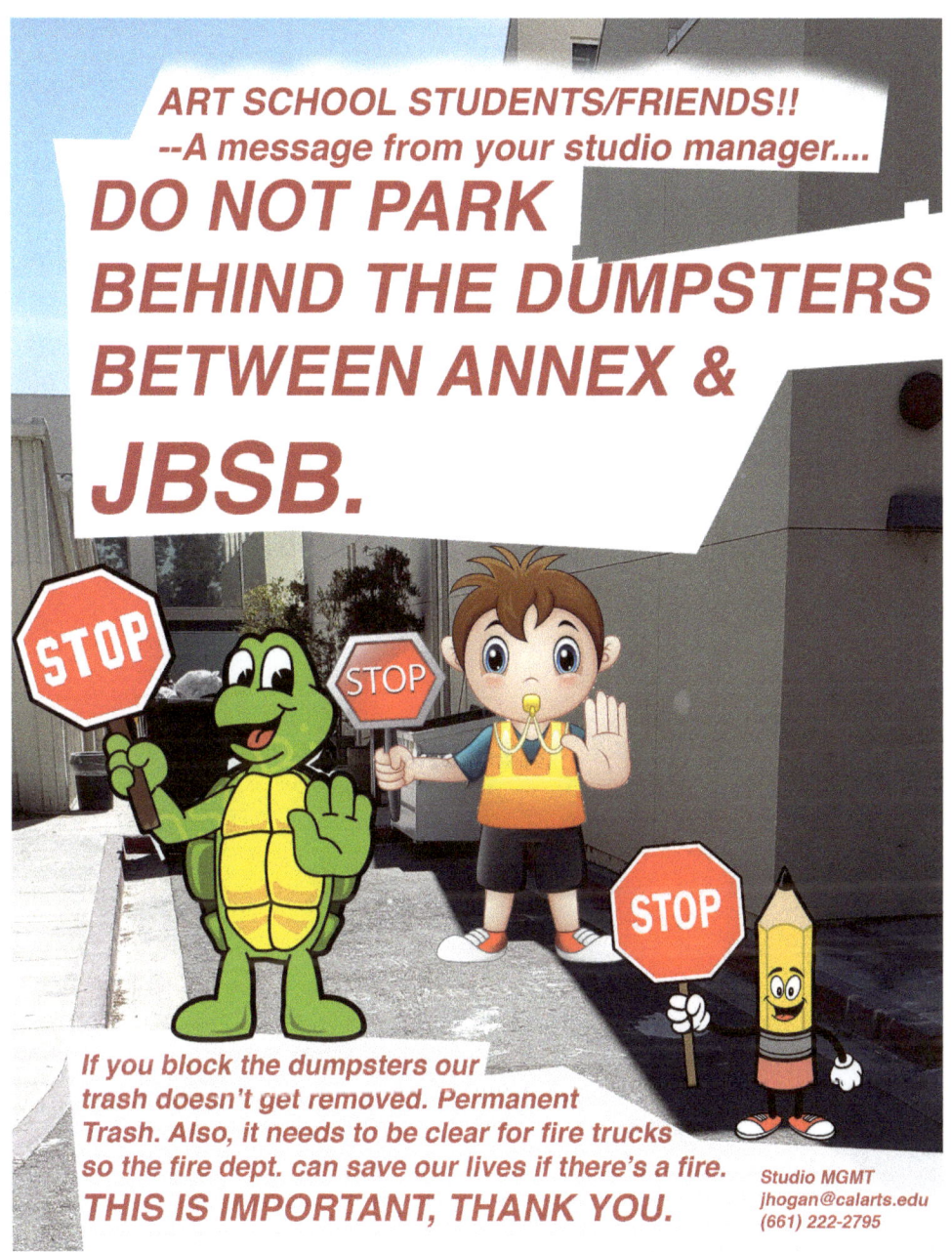

DAY-TO-DAY HECTORING

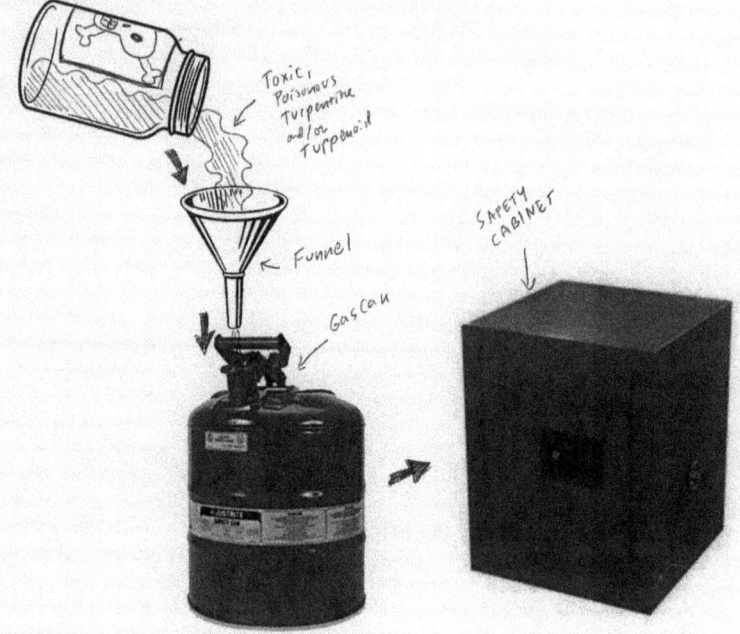

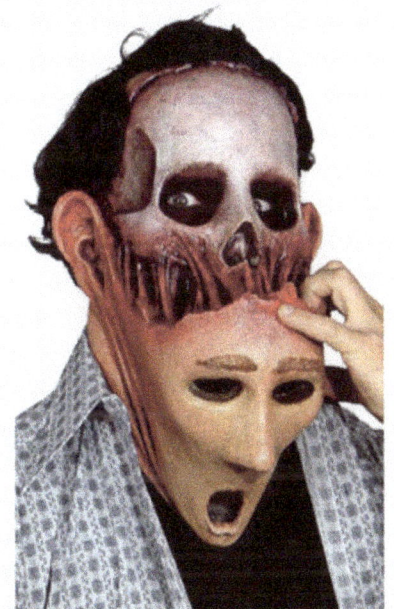

PLEASE DO NOT DRAW, WRITE, OR PAINT ON THE SIDE OF THIS OR ANY BUILDING, OK?

— J.H.

ALSO, CROSS DON'T OUT THIS "DO NOT" SO IT LOOKS LIKE I'M ASKING PEOPLE TO ACTUALLY DO THE THING I'M ASKING THEM NOT TO DO! PLEASE. THANKS.

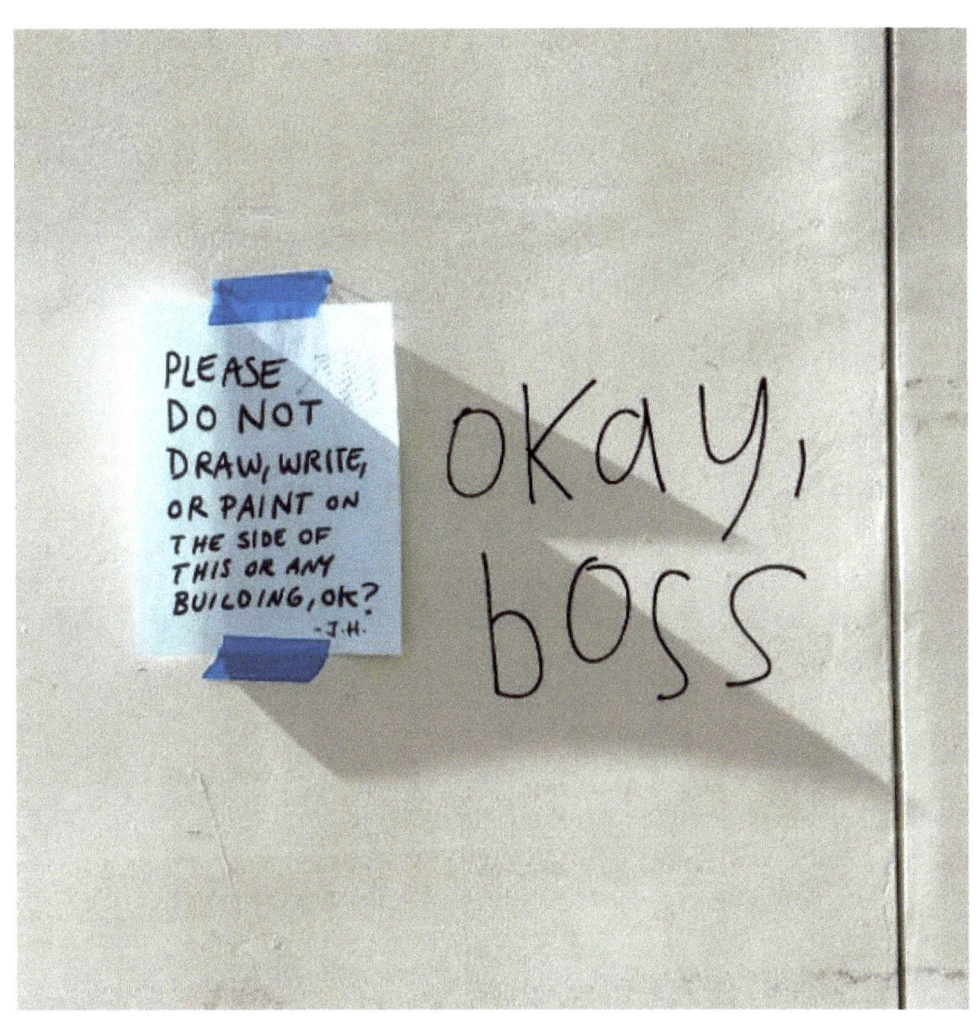

DAY-TO-DAY HECTORING

...OH YEAH AND DON'T SPRAY PAINT ON THE PAVEMENT EITHER. THIS IS ME TRYING TO BE COOL ABOUT IT RIGHT NOW.

STUDIO/GALLERY MGMT
jhogan@calarts.edu
661-222-2795

GOT SOME WORK STUDY?

Why not consider being a
GALLERY ASSISTANT?

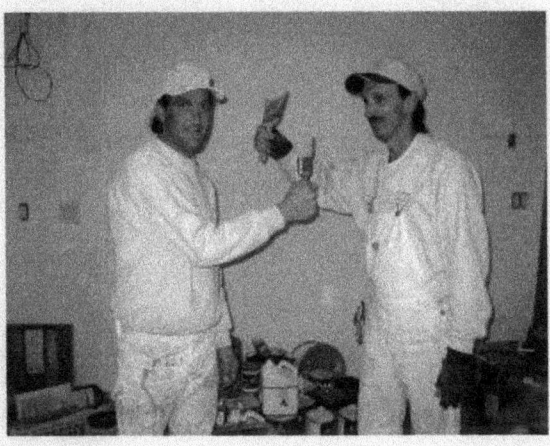

It's cooler than Silverlake, Echo Park, Highland Park, Williamsburg, Greenpoint, The Lower East Side, Wicker Park, all American Apparel stores, the iPhone, Matador Records in 1991, Jarvis Cocker in 1994, CBGB's in 1978, The MC5 in 1968, Vice Magazine in 2001, Arthur Magazine in 2006, the ghost of Kurt Cobain, Peaches, DFA remixes, The Smell, Situationism, free cable, and being able to breathe fire, all combined.

Get in on the Action.
Weekend Hours are available.

Contact John Hogan in Office A211K
Ext. 2795, jhogan@calarts.edu

So, You Want To Alter the Space and Paint The Walls A Different Color...

--well, your Studio Manager has something to say about that.

Times change. People change. Art practices change. Here's what people have been saying:

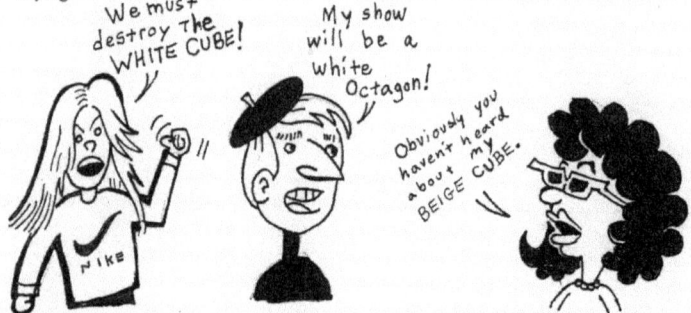

Either way. Fair enough. But before I just go and let you shift the paradigm on everyone, I've got to establish some ground rules, because things just get out of control. First of all...

ALWAYS REMEMBER: You have to return everything to the same (or better) condition as how you found it or you risk losing your deposit.

Here are some other tips:

1) **NO OIL-BASED PAINT ON WALLS, EVER.** No Exceptions.

2) **Watercolor paint, water-based markers, pastels, graphite or charcoal on wall? Wash it down w/soap and water first!** I don't like you using this stuff on the walls, and I don't want you using this stuff on the walls, but if you MUST, please wash it off before you try

and paint over it. If you put primer or house paint over this stuff without washing as much as you can off with soap and water first, you're just making life harder for yourself and everyone else.

3) Use acrylic primers KILLZ 2 and/or Bulls Eye for permanent markers and paint. Coat any drawings, paintings, etc. on the walls with this before you paint it white.

4) All of the gallery walls are painted with Dunn-Edwards Walltone W420-L Tintable White paint, and that is the exact paint that must be on the walls when you leave. Any other white is not the right white and will probably have to be painted over. Therefore, if you re-paint the walls, but just grab any old white paint off the shelf at Home Depot, that DOESN'T COUNT as returning it to it's original condition, and you could lose some or all of your deposit. An explanatory diagram can be seen below:

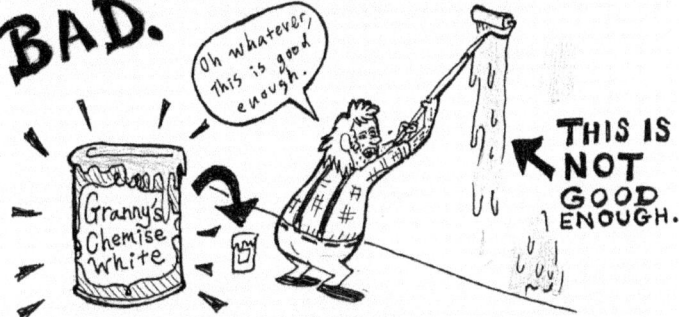

The best thing to do is to buy some paint from one of the work studies, cause all we have is W420-L over here. We'd love to sell you some, cheap! Or else go to Dunn-Edwards on the Old Road (by Wal-Mart) and ask for the W420-L at the desk. That's right. 420. You guys can remember that.

5) If you paint the walls, DO NOT PAINT OVER THE LIGHT SWITCHES!!! Trust me, your faculty and your peers will not judge you harshly if the white light switch doesn't match the otherwise nectarine-orange walls of your thesis show in the Lime Gallery. In fact, all this "painting the light switch" phenomenon tells me is that people have forgotten about this stuff called TAPE. You can totally TAPE OFF THE LIGHT SWITCH and avoid my wrath. I will always consider your painting of the light switch as a blatant affront to CalArts property and to myself, personally, and this will be reflected in how much of your gallery deposit you get back.

6) GIVE YOURSELF TIME TO FINISH THE JOB. I know, I know. Thursday night you drank 11 Tecates, 2 bottles of Charles Show Merlot, 4 Jaegermeister shots, smoked a carton of cigarettes and ate a possum you found in the dumpster. You needed Friday to recover. But now it's Saturday afternoon and you painted all 1,240 square feet of wallspace in D300 Kelly Green! You've only got 6 hours before that disgruntled MFA2 is coming in expecting the walls to be perfectly, absolutely white so he can video-project modulations of chromatic gray on them for the thesis project he's been working on for 2 years! Barring a miracle, you screwed yourself and you are out (at least) 50 bucks and will be privy to a whole lot of passive (or non-passive) aggression from somebody else. Remember, ambition of scale requires temperance of self (or something, I don't know, but just remember it takes a long time to get the walls white and to clean things up). If the Studio Manager (me) has to clean up after you, he will only do so after bothering you a lot on the phone, after which, if you do not finish the job, your name will live in infamy and you may not *only* lose your deposit, but might *also* end up paying for the extra labor costs.

But Hey, Look, I DON'T WANT TO STRESS YOU OUT!

WE'RE HERE TO HELP !
(within reason)

Feel free to contact ME with any questions or problems.

Sincerely,

John Hogan
Studio Manager
Art Department
Office A211K
(661) 222-2795
X. 2795 on-campus.

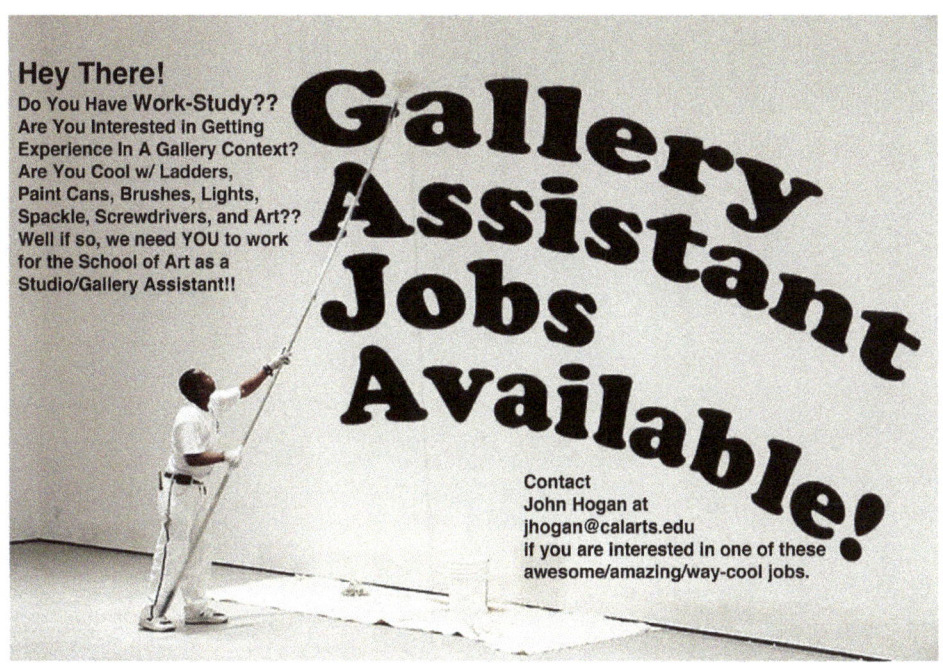

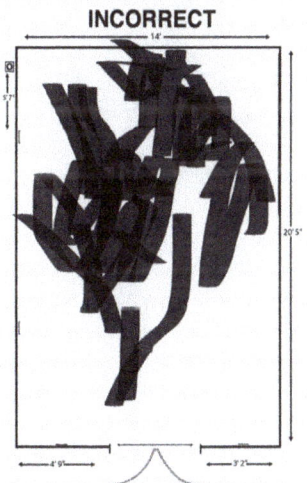

DAY-TO-DAY HECTORING / 71

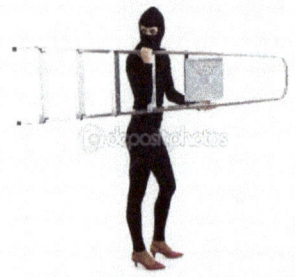

SORRY GUYS, BUT...
Due to Recurring
<u>LADDER LOSS</u>
WE WILL NO LONGER LEND OUT LADDERS OVER NIGHT.
The Gallery Ladder MUST be returned to gallery storage closet by <u>6pm DAILY</u>.

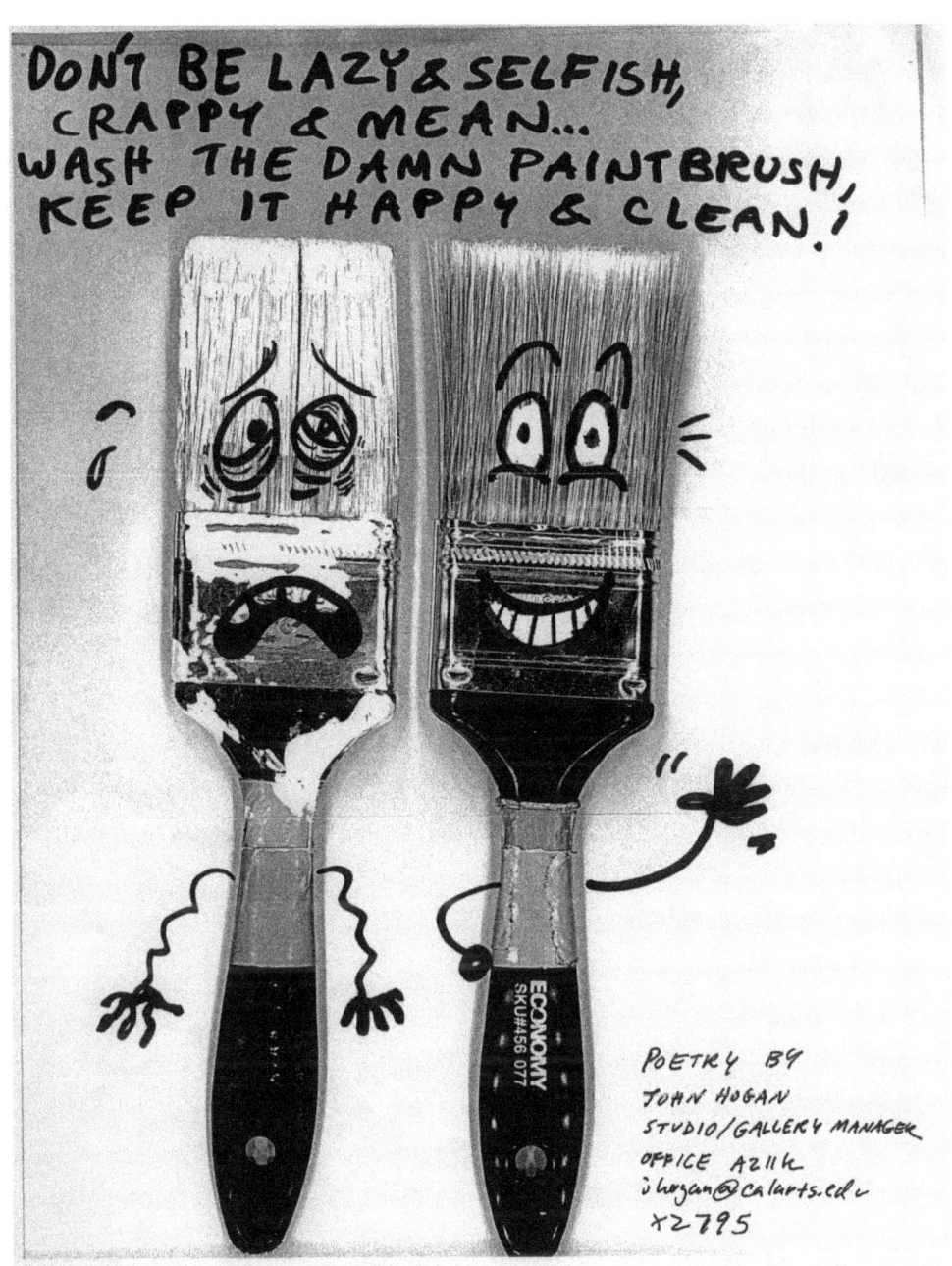

DAY-TO-DAY HECTORING / 73

THE TOILET IS TIRED.

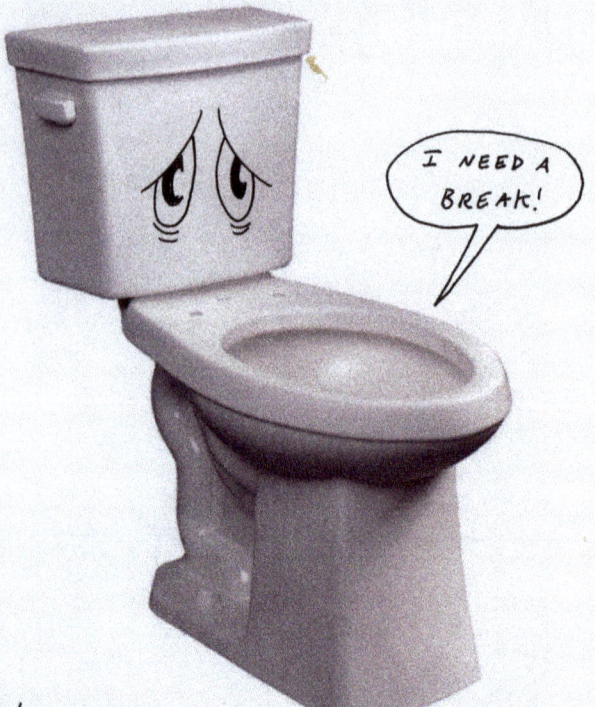

I NEED A BREAK!

You may have noticed the Toilets in the Annex are almost always backing up. We suspect this may have to do with the <u>high traffic</u> they are receiving. These bathrooms are only meant to serve students w/ studios in the <u>Annex</u> and <u>Broads</u>. Please do NOT USE This Restroom if your class or studio is located in C-Art (JBSB) or C-Block (C116, C114, C111, C107, Ceramics Area) the C-Block has its own, large, un-exhausted restrooms over by the stairs. If you have a studio in Annex or Broads, Please do NOT Leave doors to the ANNEX PROPPED OPEN! THANK YOU! — Studio Mgmt, x2795

PLEASE DO NOT USE THE BBQ

DURING SANTA ANA WINDS.

THANK YOU!

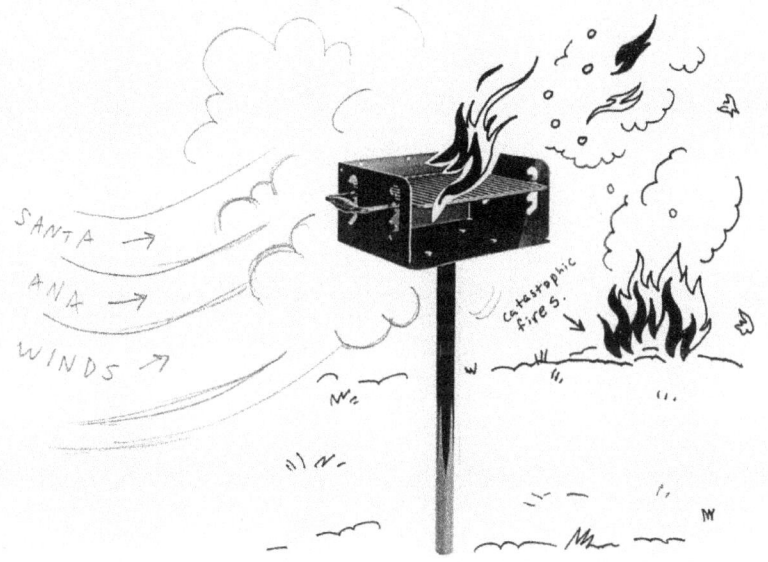

Studio/Gallery Mgmt
Office A211k
jhogan@calarts.edu
(661) 222-2795

IF YOU NEED TO
SPRAY-PAINT SOME-
THING PLEASE DO
THE COURTEOUS AND
ENVIRONMENTALLY
RESPONSIBLE THING
AND USE THE SPRAY
BOOTH IN THE
SUPERSHOP.
THANKS!!

STUDIO/GALLERY MGMT
(661) 222-2795
JHOGAN@CALARTS.EDU

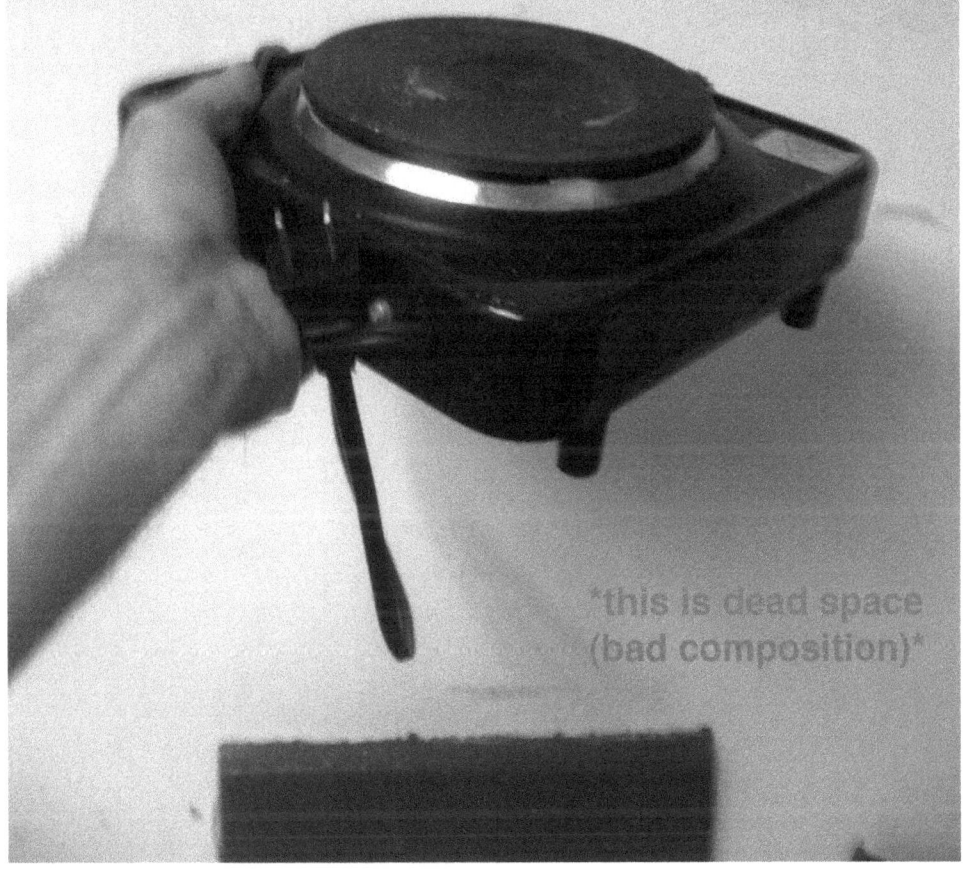

DAY-TO-DAY HECTORING / 77

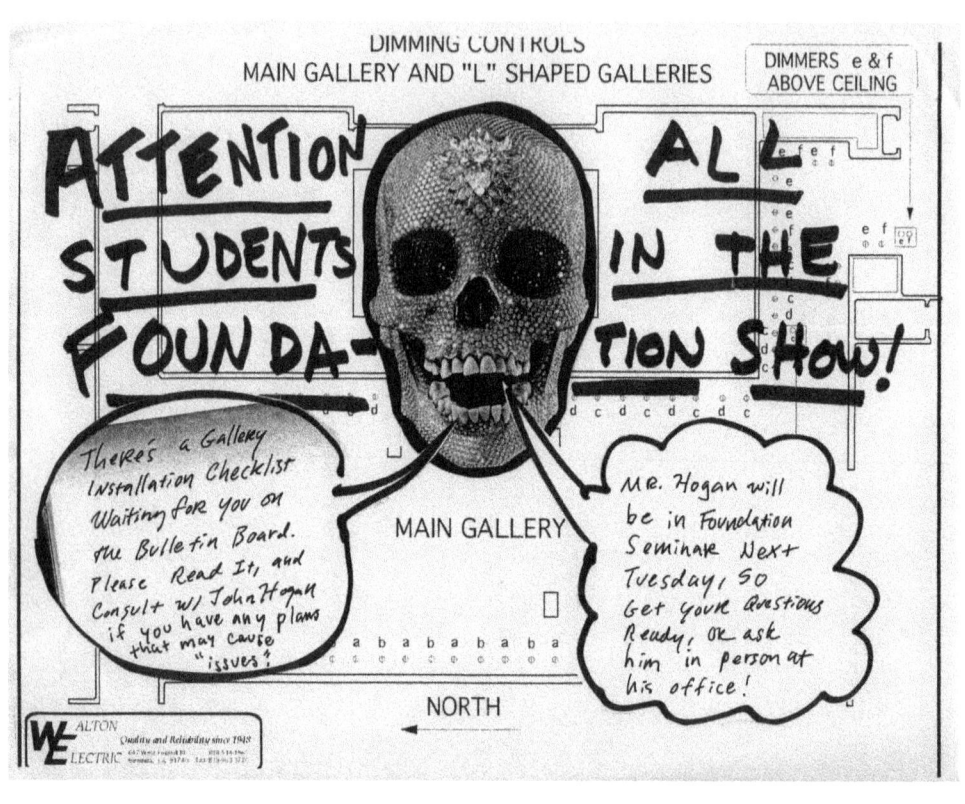

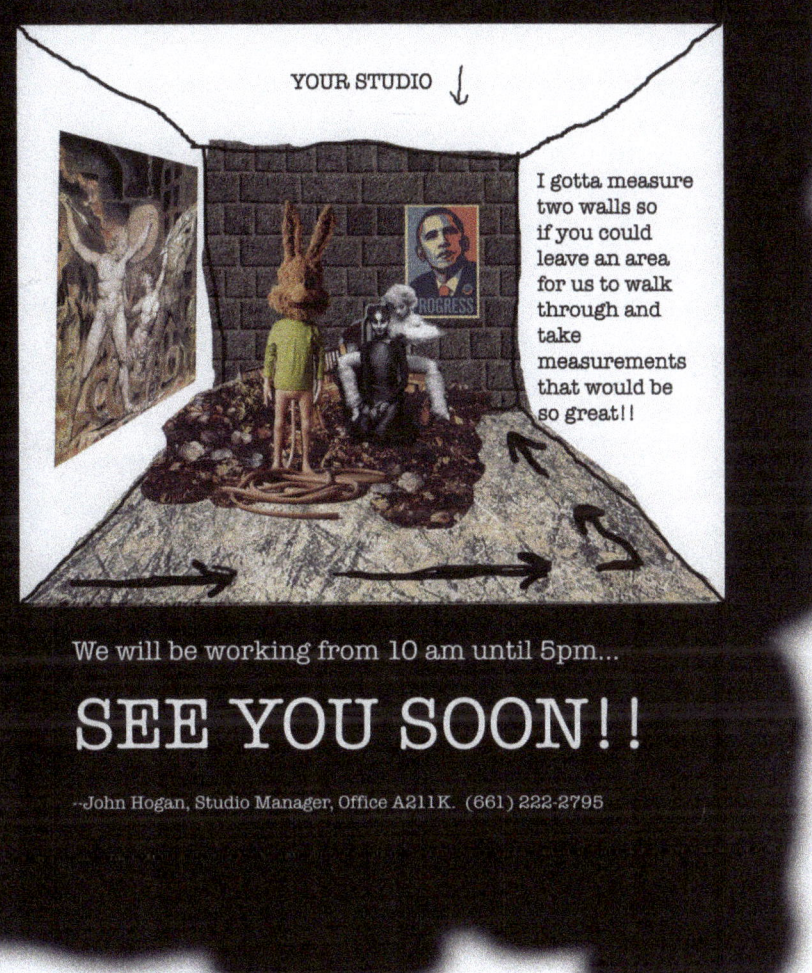

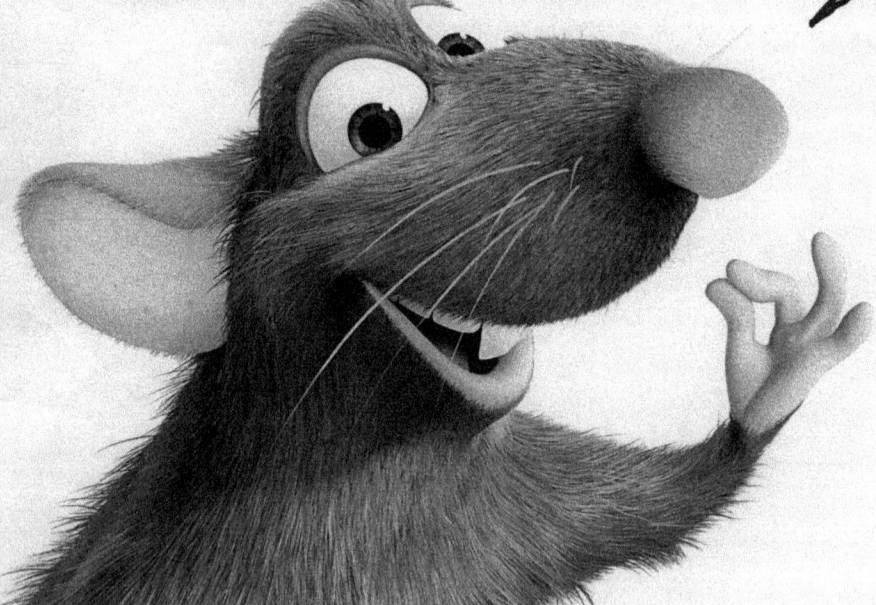

HEY!

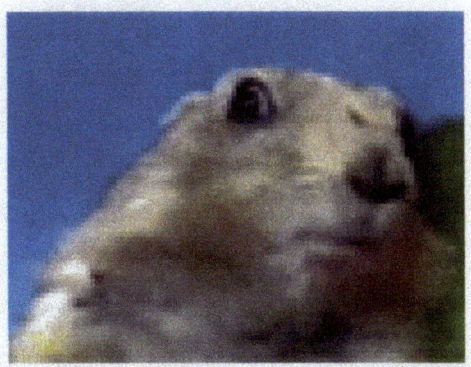

IS THIS ART, OR IS IT ART SUPPLIES, OR IS IT TRASH?
I NEED TO KNOW, OR ELSE IT WILL TURN INTO TRASH NEXT WEEK!

THANKS,

JOHN HOGAN
Studio Manager
Office A211K
jhogan@calarts.edu
661-222-2795

SUMMERTIME

Summer's Coming!

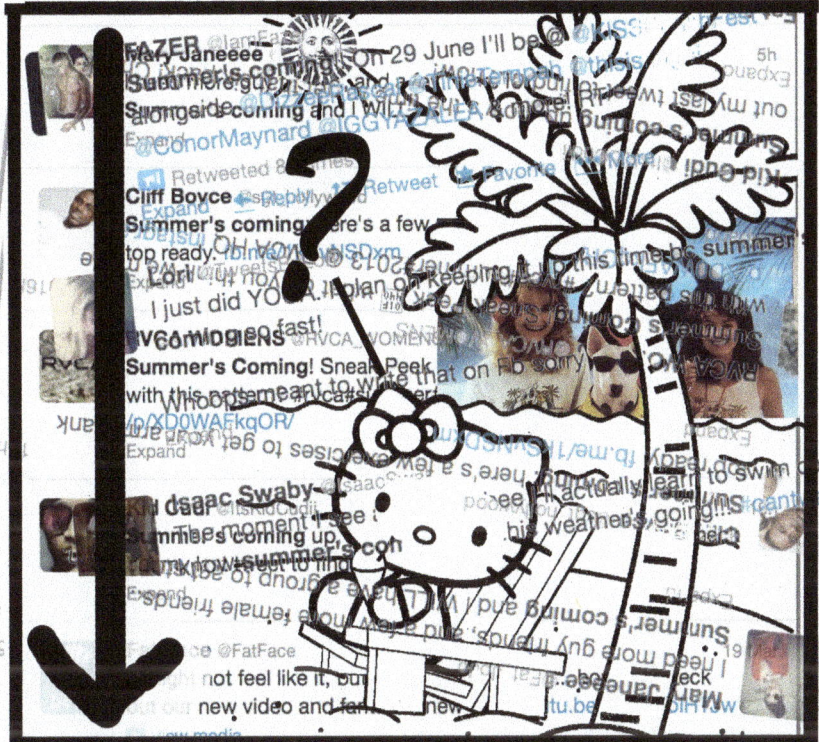

Summer Studio Info & Applications Are Coming To You! Check your school mailbox. If you don't Apply, you have 0% chance of receiving a Summer Studio! Applications Are Due April 12th!!!!!

—John Hogan, Studio/Gallery Manager, Office A211K, 661-222-2795, jhogan@calarts.edu

SUMMER STUDIO PAP[ER] INFORMATION SESSIO[N]

If you want to rent a studio this summer you have to go to one of these meetings to get the application!

...with you.
STUDIO M[ANAGER]
JOHN HO[GAN]
jhogan@c[...]

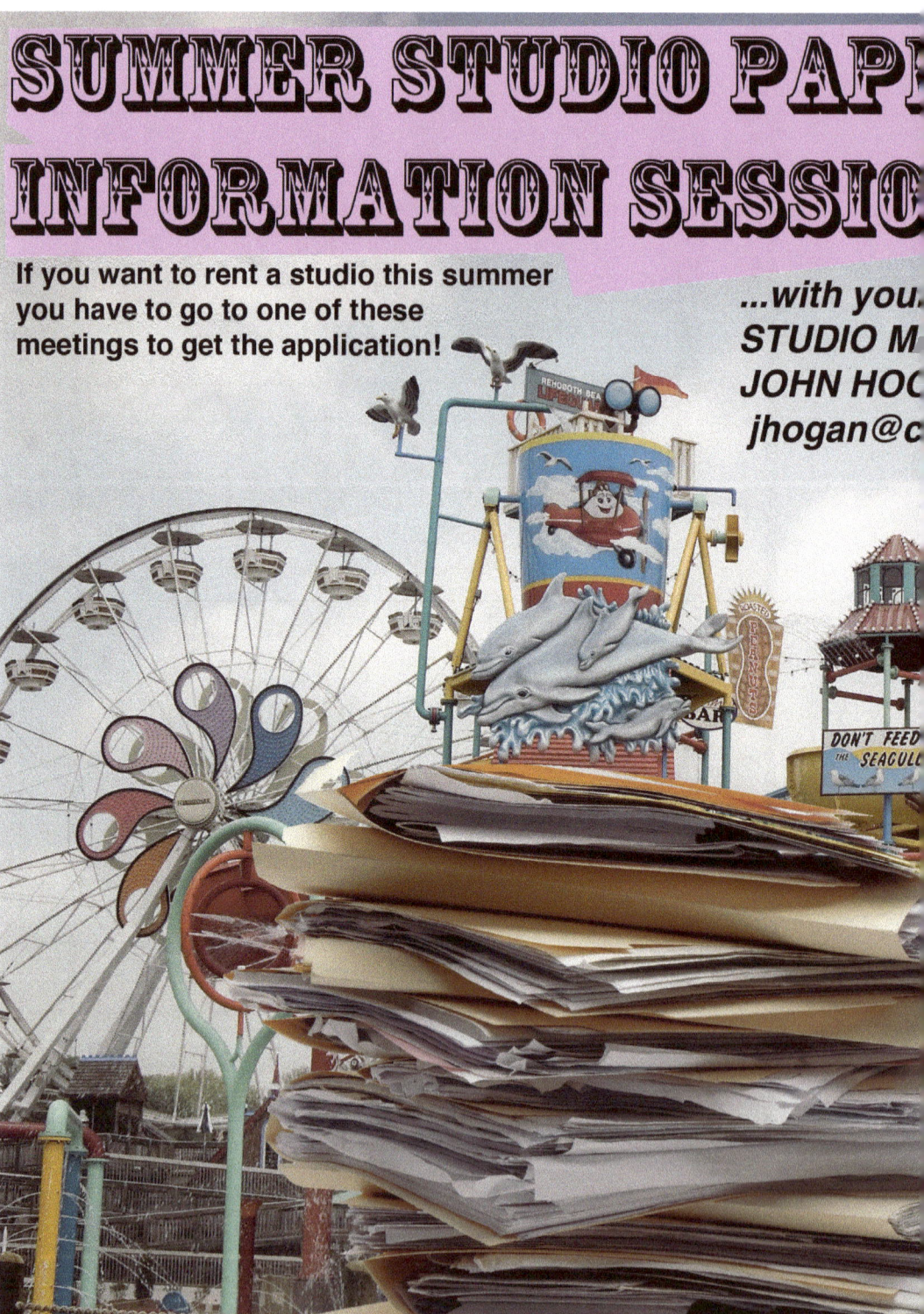

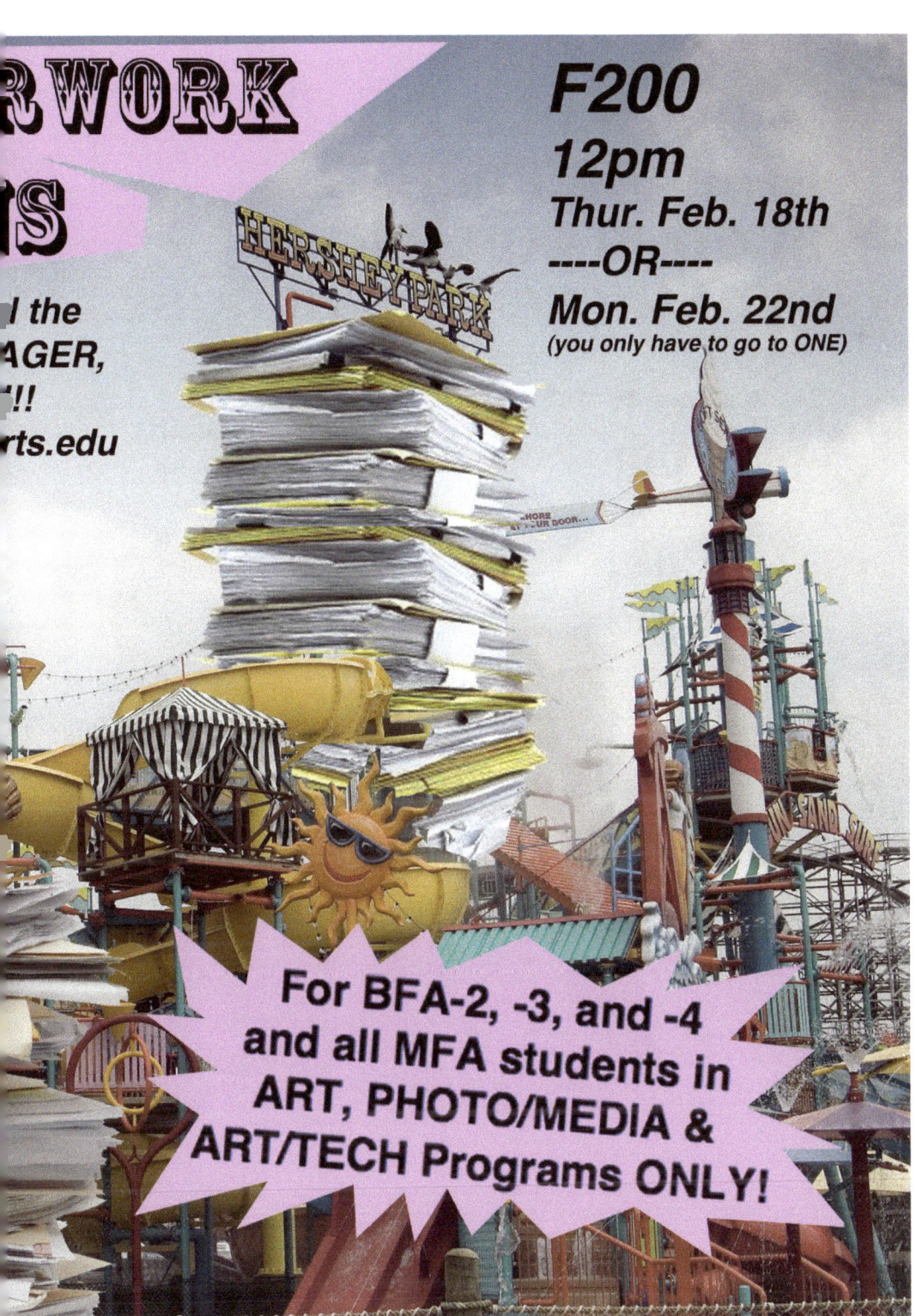

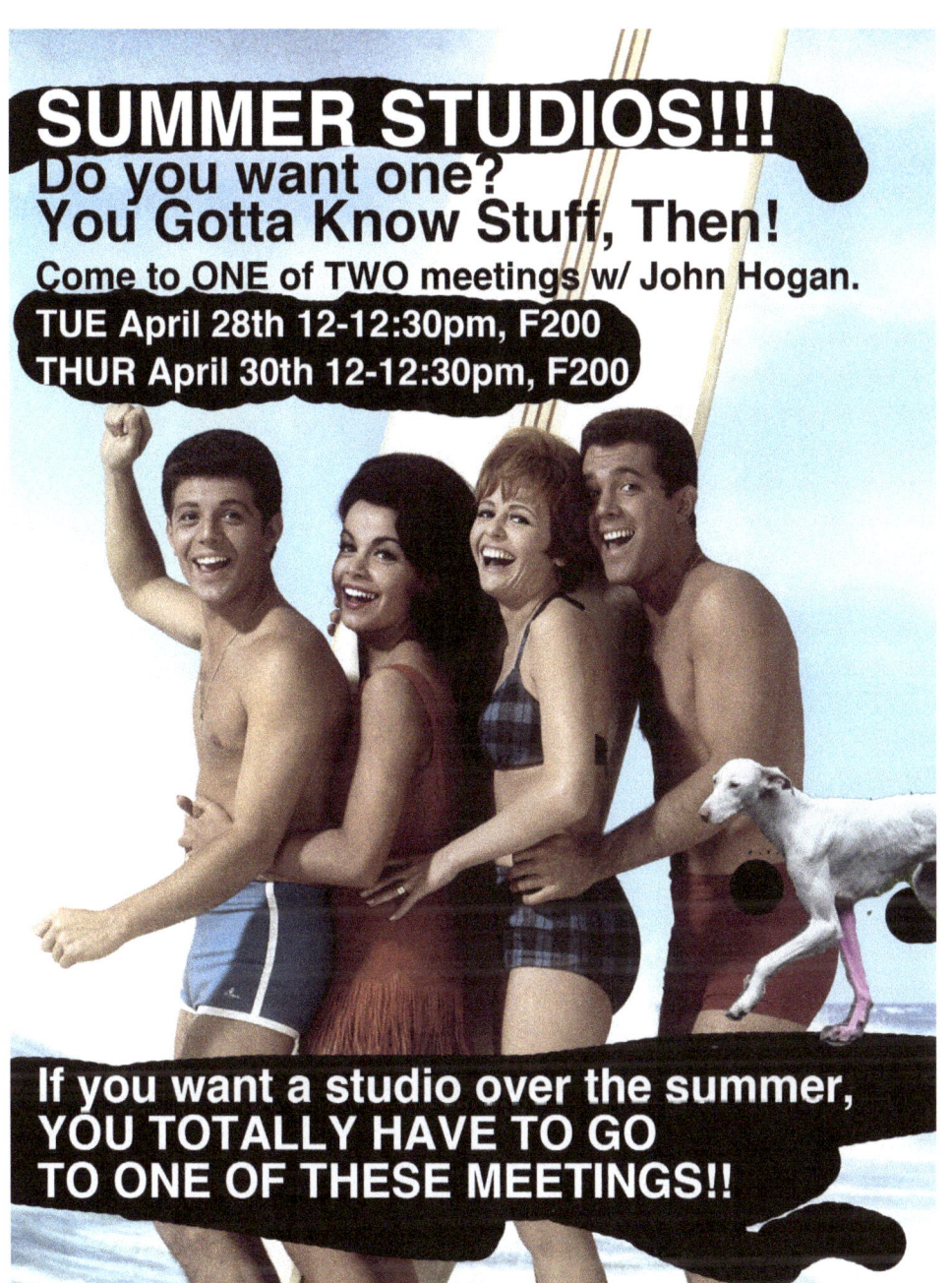

AS OF MAY 14th
I AM NO LONGER ACCEPTING ANY LATE SUMMER STUDIO PAPERWORK.

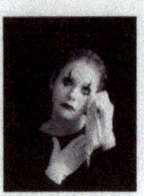

THANKS, JOHN HOGAN

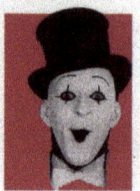

The only exceptions are people who I've spoken to *before* May 14th and made special arrangements with.

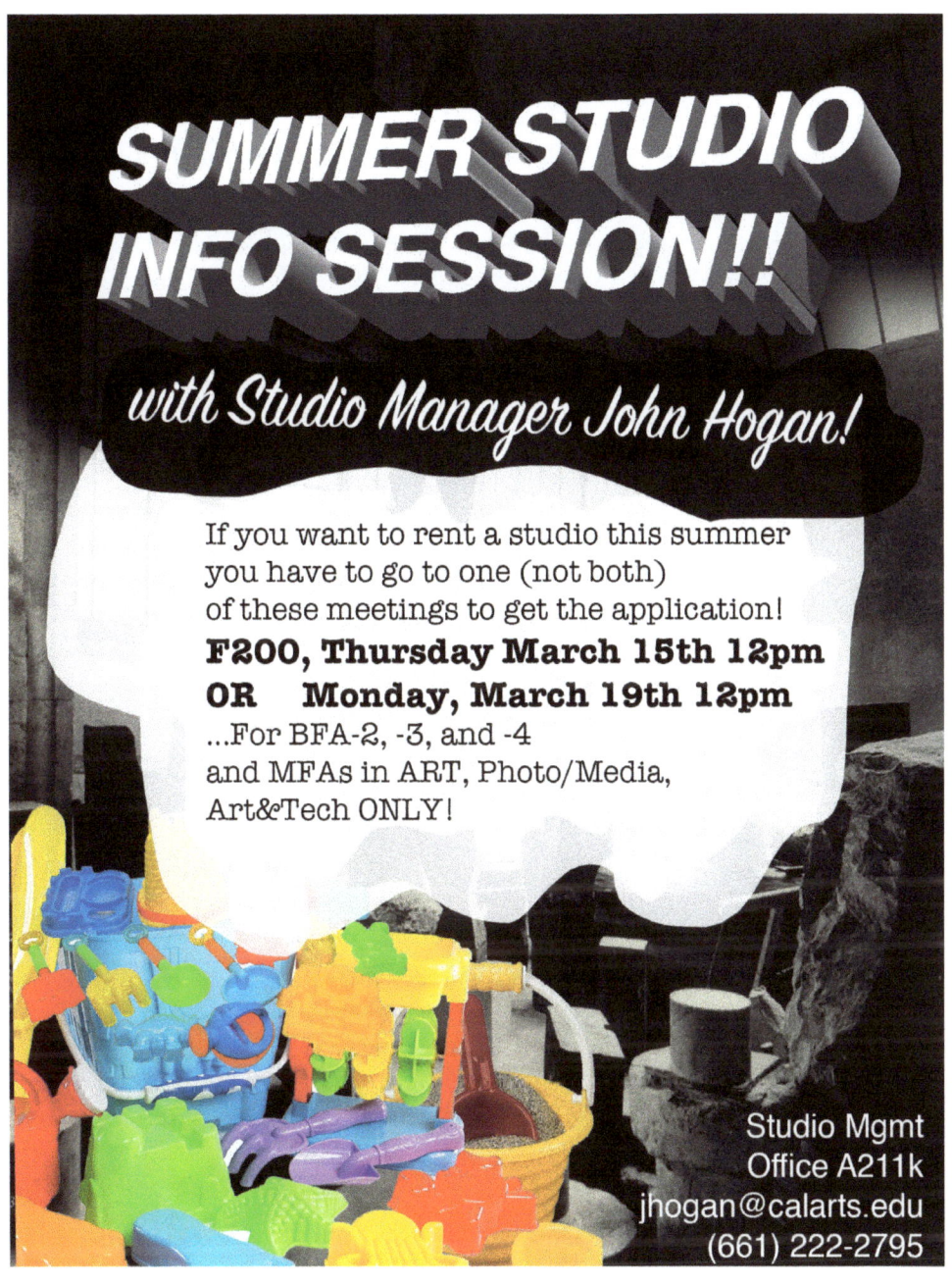

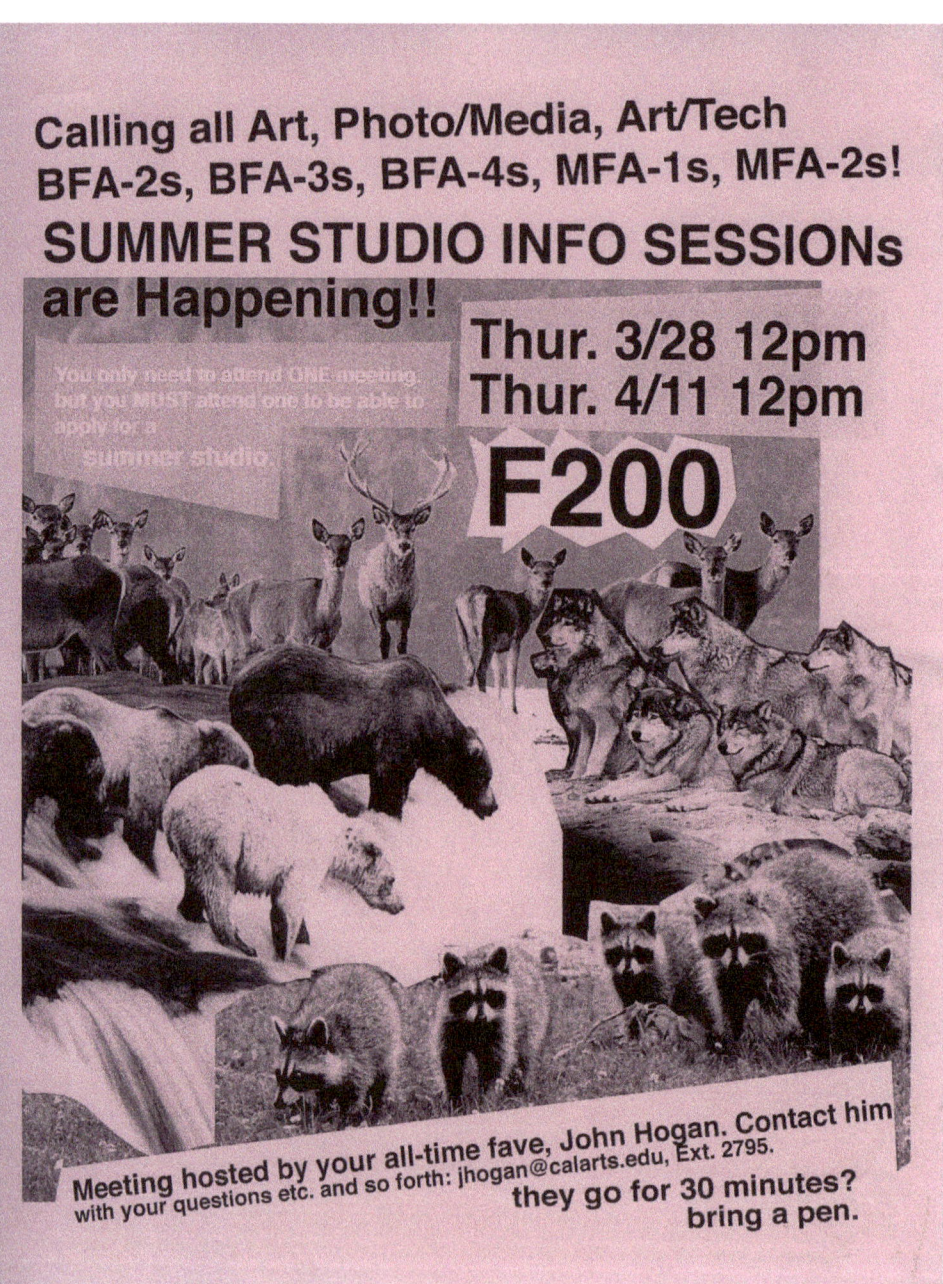

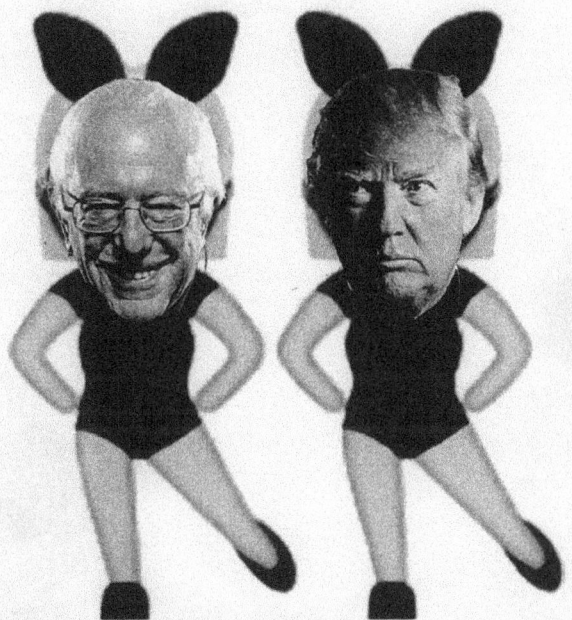

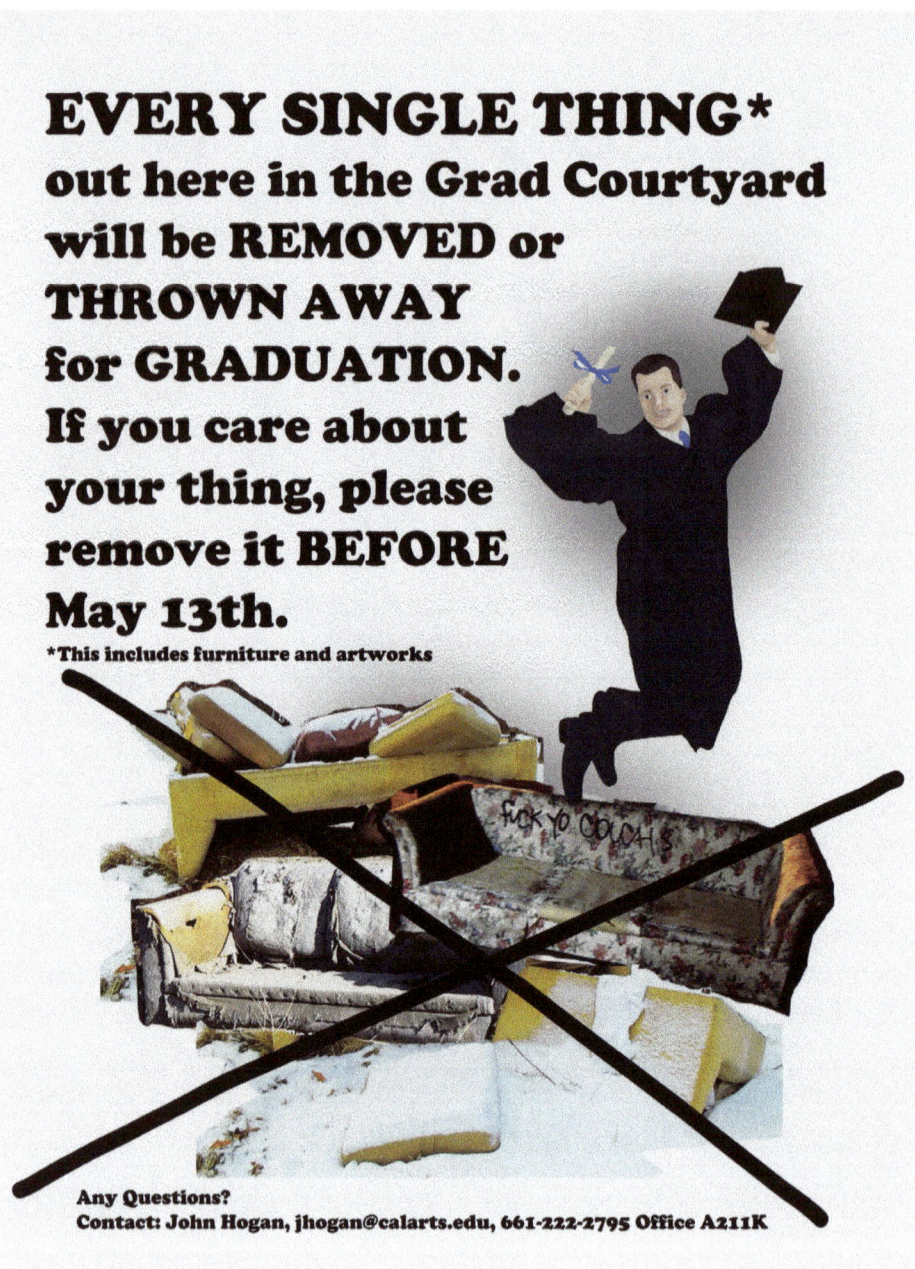

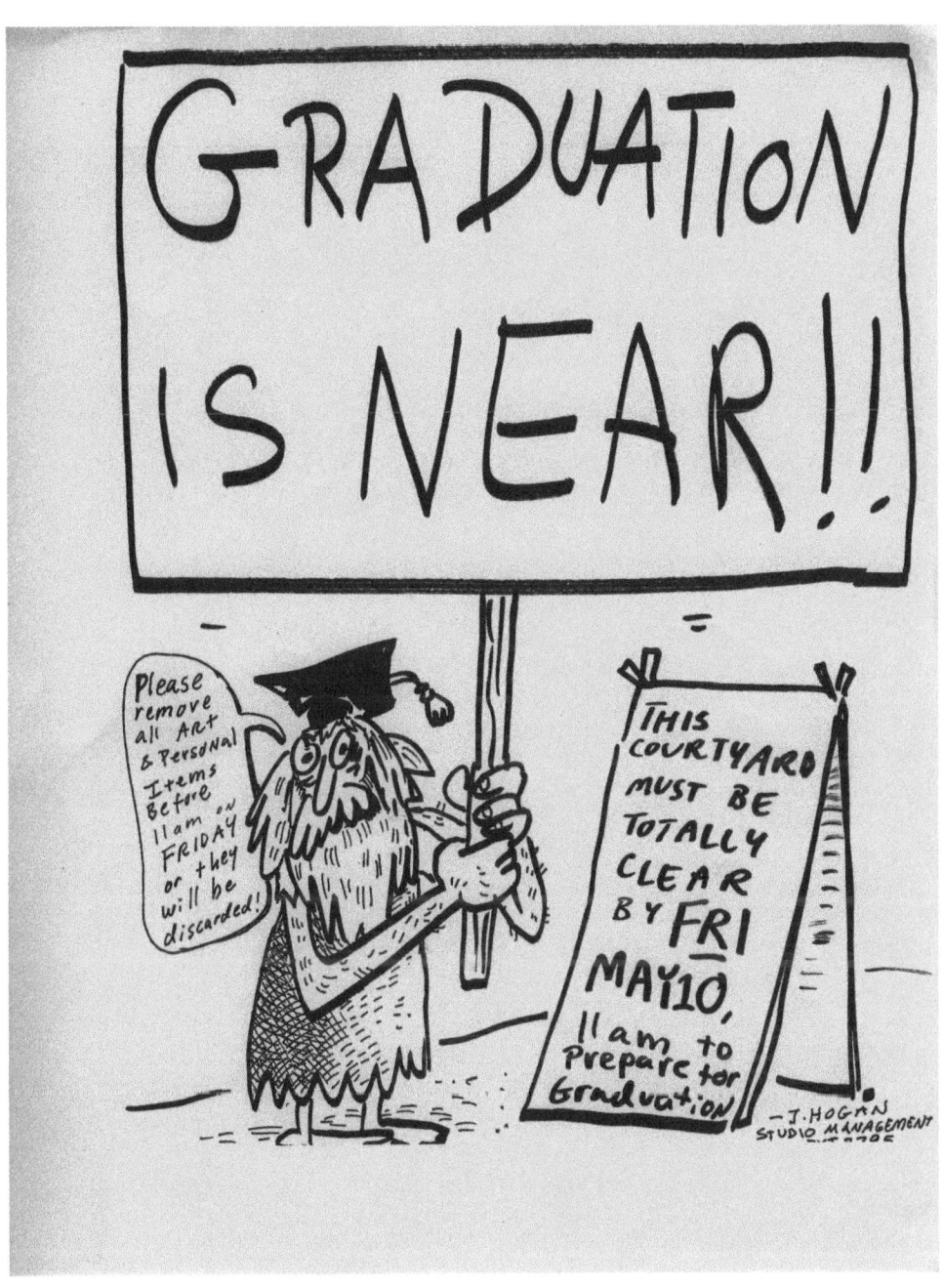

MOVE-OUT NOTICES

MFA-2's:
YOU MUST MOVE IN TO YOUR NEW STUDIOS <u>BEFORE</u> MONDAY, 9/20.

DON'T THINK ABOUT IT...

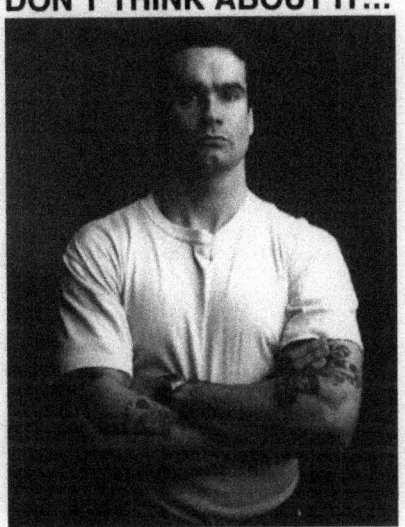

DO IT.

MFA-1's in Art will get their new studio keys on Monday. There's your motivation.

John Hogan
Studio/Gallery Manager
Office A211K
jhogan@calarts.edu

TIME'S UP!

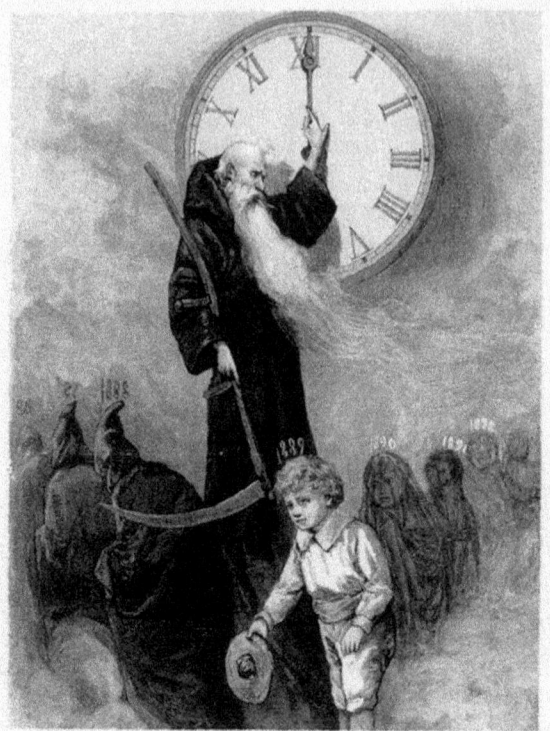

Please clear out all personal items from this room by Monday, June 2nd, or they will be THROWN AWAY.

A message from John Hogan, Studio Manager, Office A211K, jhogan@calarts.edu, (661) 222-2795

People who have graduated must move out of studios by
FRI, AUGUST 16th

It's kinda sad, but it'll be okay. Please patch all walls and return them to white. Please throw all trash in Institute dumpsters. Please do not leave trash in studio or hallways.

Studio/Gallery Mgmt.
(661) 222-2795
jhogan@calarts.edu

TIME TO MOVE

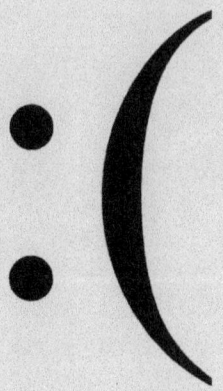

IF YOU HAVE GRADUATED AND ARE STILL IN YOUR STUDIO
**PLEASE MOVE OUT
AS SOON AS POSSIBLE**.

THE OFFICIAL MOVE-OUT DATE WAS AUGUST 1ST.

Thanks,
Studio Manager
Office A211K
jhogan@calarts.edu
661-222-2795

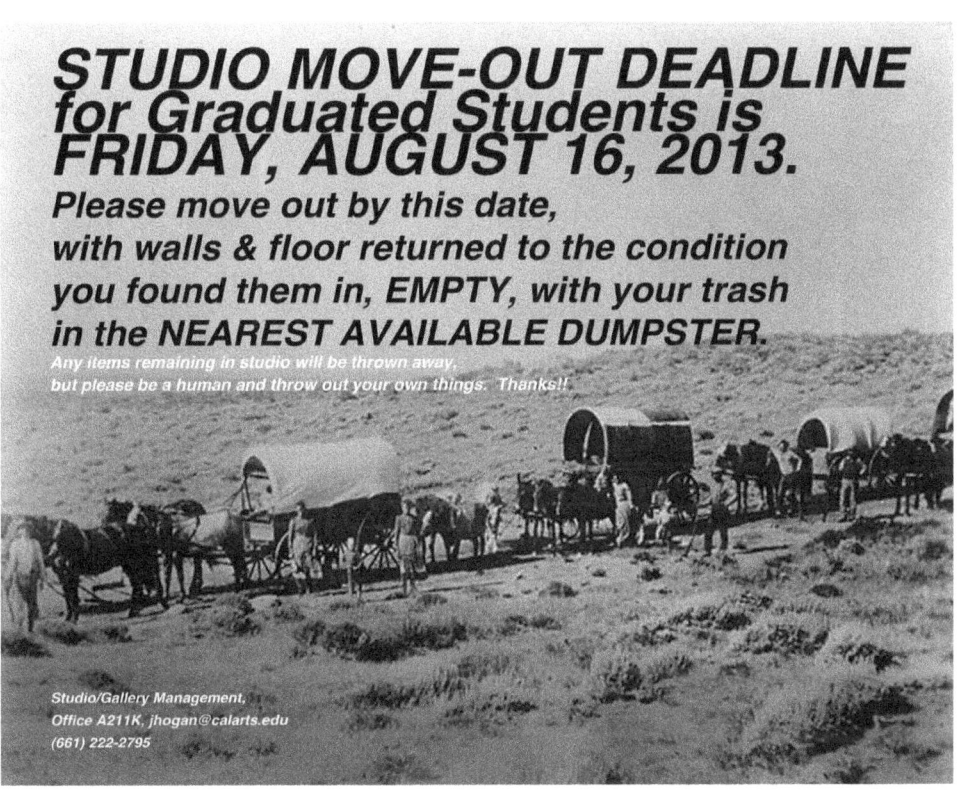

Issue Date:_____

THAT'S IT!! YOU NEED TO MOVE OUT!

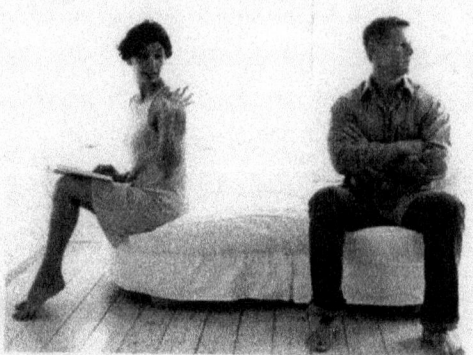

You've got a new studio. That studio is ready for you and is perfectly good. It's feeling neglected and wants you to use it. Why don't you want to move in to your new studio???

You've got an old studio (This One). This studio has already moved on. It's ready for the new tenant. The new tenant is ready for IT, and in fact neither can wait for you to move out. Please let this studio begin its new life. Honestly, the time you shared with this studio was special, but nothing lasts forever and we both know hearts can change.

PLEASE MOVE OUT OF THIS STUDIO AND INTO YOUR NEW ONE AS SOON AS POSSIBLE!

THANKS!!
JOHN HOGAN
Studio Manager
Office A211K
Ext. 2795
jhogan@calarts.edu

GRAD CRIT ROOM (A112-D) STORAGE

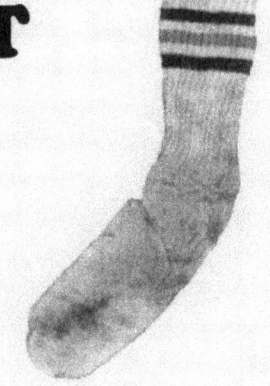

OPEN TODAY, FRI. May 21st
11AM – 3PM
(or until it becomes obvious no one is going to show up anymore)

You must have completed and turned in your storage paperwork & $25 receipt to John Hogan BEFORE you put stuff in A112-D. This paperwork was emailed to all graphic design undergrads and yellow copies of it were left on everyone's desk.

All items in storage must be labeled with your name and contact information.

Any questions or problems contact John Hogan: jhogan@calarts.edu, Office A211k, jhogan@calarts.edu

DELEGATIONS
&
COLLABORATIONS

Hey! Your friend Wilson the volleyball has something to say!

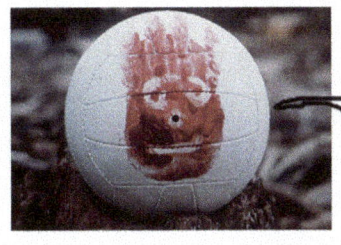

Don't forget to fill out your

SUMMER STUDIO APPLICATION!!!!!!!!!

-- and return it to John Hogan's office A211k

IT'S DUE

APRIL 19th!

There's a form in your mailbox & email!!!

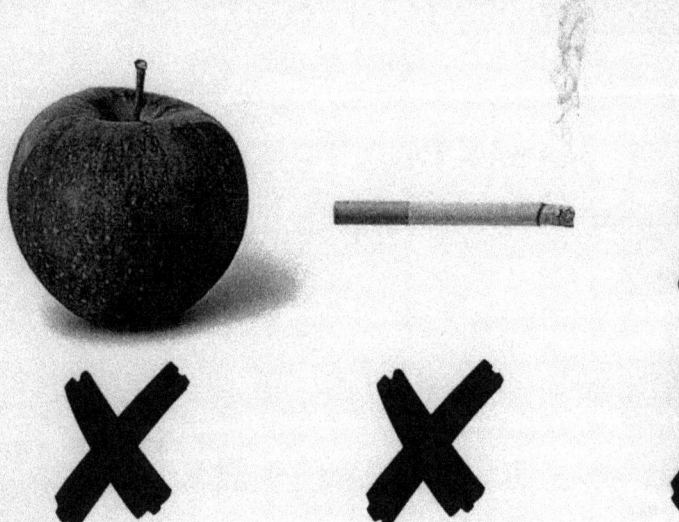

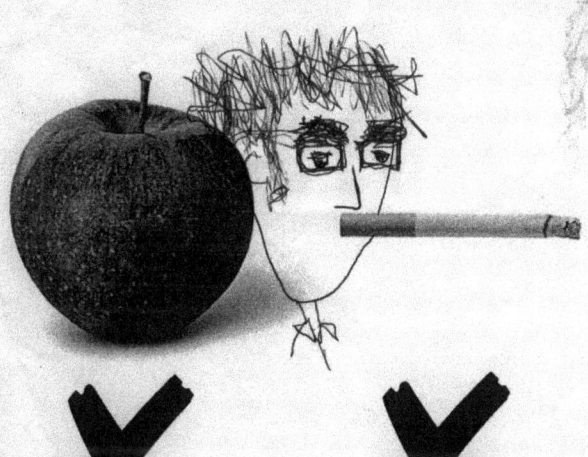

WARNING: WET FLOOR

PLEASE

BE CAREFUL

✱ GALLERY MANAGEMENT

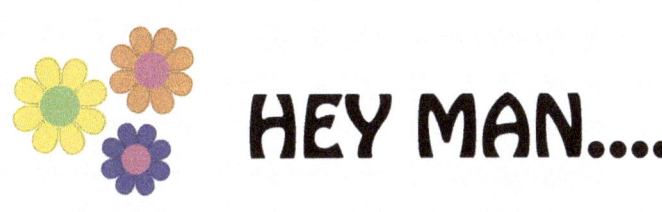
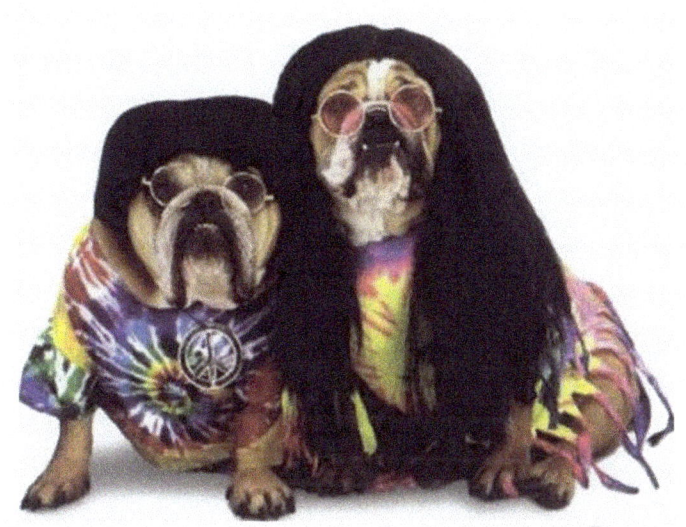

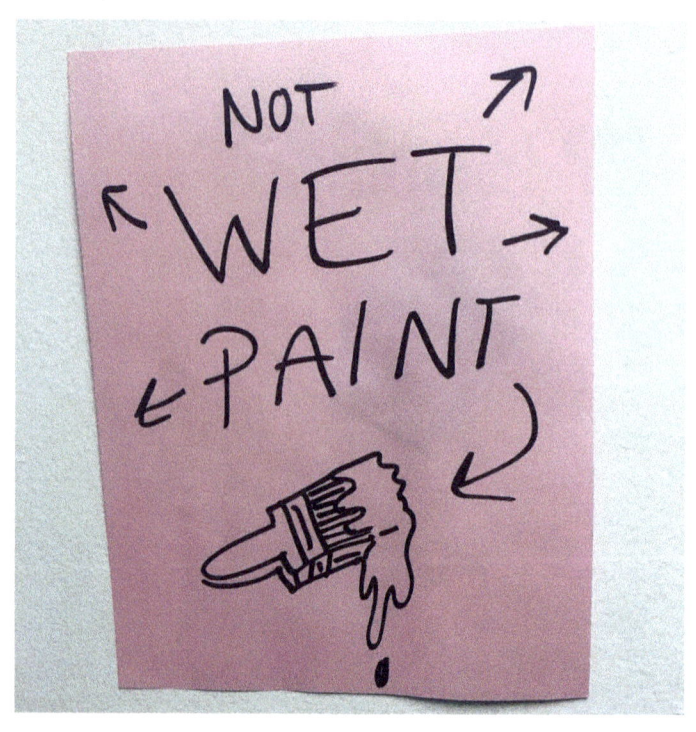
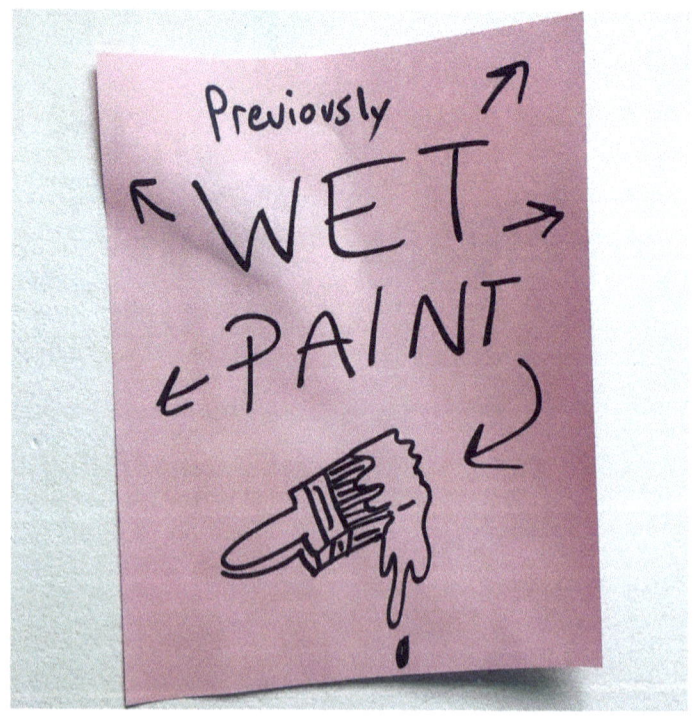

BODY PAINTING @ 9 PM

12/13/18

in BB6

(Out by the last parking lot, down the hill from the Generator Bldg)

Streak
@ 10 PM
12/13/18

Meet here in
the Main Gal

Body painting @ 9PM
in BB6

PLATE INFORMATION

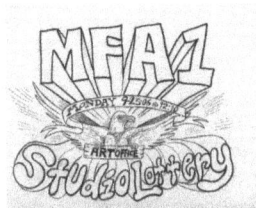

MFA-1 Studio Lottery September 2006, page 33
My first ever flyer for CalArts was a meticulous ink drawing announcing the MFA studio lotteries. The studio lotteries are the first phase of indoctrination to the CalArts Art Program, at turns cruel and exhilarating. This work is fussy and its ambition exceeds its function. Aesthetically speaking, charming failure!

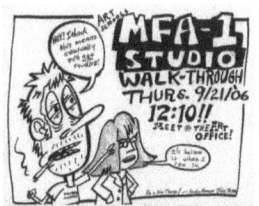

MFA-1 Studio Walk-Through September 2006, page 33
I remember creating this right after the lottery flyer, having suddenly remembered I had to do a tour with the Art MFAs before the lottery itself, so I scheduled the tour and created the flyer in great haste. You can tell the significant drop in quality, yet the spirit of all forthcoming flyers comes into clearer view. The slapdash production, the defensive tone, and the not-quite veiled contempt for grad students and their impatience.

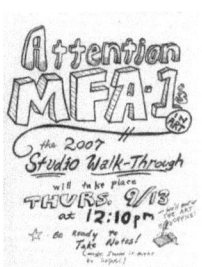

Attention MFA-1s September 2007, page 34
Another hand-drawn flyer in the style of underground comics. By my second year, I've already shed the editorial content in favor of a single pen writing a note on paper in the bottom right hand corner.

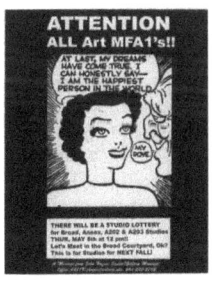

My Dove 2007, page 35
I suppose I used this decontextualized panel from an old *Dick Tracy* comic to gently poke fun at the notion that graduate school and an institutional art studio had the potential to improve your life. Assessing this now in the context of my personal timeline, it would seem I was Immediately bitter about my art career not exploding the moment I got that diploma in hand. Anyway, this flyer looked good from far away.

The Lottery 2014, page 36
Here is a high-concept studio lottery flyer that references *The Lottery*, a 1969 horror film in which the "winner" of the lottery receives a black spot on a piece of paper. I think they get murdered? But hold on, that's not all, there is a shocking twist to this story...

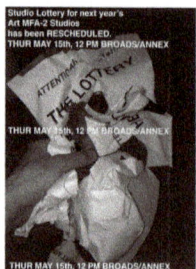

The Lottery: Revised 2014, page 37
I had to reschedule the lottery and so the original The Lottery flyer had to be destroyed. A photo of its crumpled and twisted corpus became the basis for the new flyer with the corrected schedule.

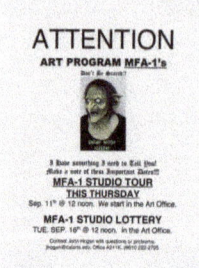

ATTENTION Witch 2009, page 38
I am hazy about when exactly this was made, but I do recall that, at this time, I had gotten it into my head that people were afraid of me and there was a sense of dread about seeing my name attached to things. I attempted to subvert this phenomenon by putting a scary witch mask on the Studio Walk-Through flyer and putting the phrase "Don't Be Scared" on it.

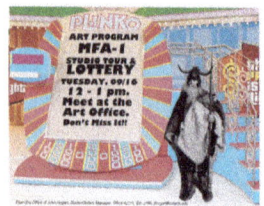

Studio Lottery (Moondog) 2014, page 39
The Art and Photo/Media programs have different studio lotteries, and those programs have different vibes. Art is more rough-and-tumble classic bohemian, Photo/Media is more cosmopolitan futuristic. Art is like the Grateful Dead, Photo/Media is Kraftwerk. In this flyer, "Art Program" is represented by visionary avant garde twentieth century composer Moondog, at the Plinko machine on the set of The Price Is Right.

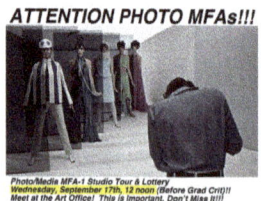

Blow Up 2014, page 39
Whereas the Photo/Media flyer that same year was an appropriated still from Antonioni's *Blow Up*, because the guy's a photographer, and also because Photo/Media students are generally more cosmopolitan sophisticates with good clothes.

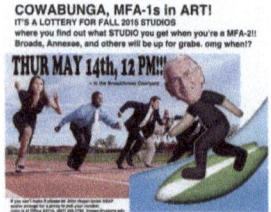

Cowabunga (Eli Broad) 2016, page 40
We have these studios called The Broad studios and they're named after donor Eli Broad. They're the nicest studios on campus, so here's a flyer of some people in business clothes about to run a race, they're sort of racing toward Eli Broad who's depicted with his own head on an emoji surfer because emojis were very much in the zeitgeist at the time. I also wanted to goof around with the image of Eli Broad, who was a major patron of the arts, as well as a diabolical monomaniac capitalist.

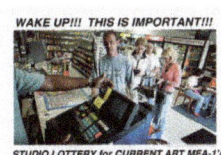

Wake Up!!! 2013, page 40
An attempt to rouse MFAs from their late-spring torpor to take part in a lottery that will decide all their fates. It becomes difficult to get their attention after Spring Break, as the pressures and stresses of the year have destroyed psyches and livers.

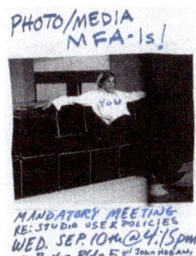

Black Couch 2015, page 41
Further stereotyping of the Photo/Media student in my mind led to this almost accusatory flyer meant to summon them to a meeting about studio safety.

Lottery Balls 2013, page 42
When I was very young and growing up in New Jersey, my parents would watch the Pick 6 Lotto drawings on TV and they would get so into it (they also liked to go to "the track" and Atlantic City). I understood their feelings related to the lottery as 100% positive and unproblematic fun, and the lottery balls spinning around as objects of magical fascination.

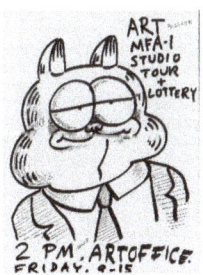

Garfield 1 2017, page 43
My thinking here was "I've been able to draw Garfield since I was four years old, what if that was a flyer?"

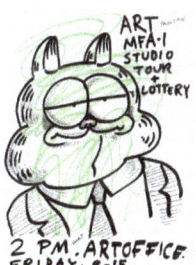

Garfield 2 2017, page 44
My thinking here was "What if I put green highlighter all over this Garfield flyer?"

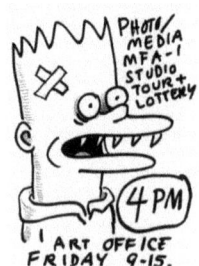

Bart 2017, page 45
And my thinking here was "What if it was Bart... But edgy?!"

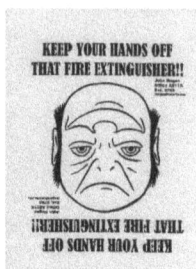

Keep Your Hands Off That Fire Extinguisher 2006, page 47
When I first started, we had a rash of people letting off fire extinguishers, and someone (another person presumably) who would turn all the flyers upside down. So I made a few flyers that were the same upside down and right side up. I just took these brain-teaser designs from the internet and made them the image, and put the type at the top, and the same type upside down at the bottom, so it would always say what I wanted it to.

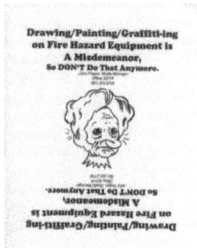

Don't Do That Anymore 2006, page 48
Upside down rightside up face.

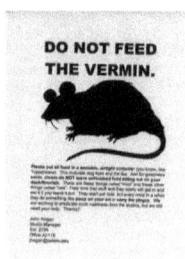

Do Not Feed The Vermin 2007-2008, page 49
There was a rat problem in the graphic design studios being exacerbated by students storing open boxes of cereal and bags of pet food in their cubicles. The rats have Mickey Mouse ears as a nod to the Disney history of CalArts, I guess. At this time, I was reading a lot of David Foster Wallace and I felt that a glut of copy signified sophistication and hipness or something. I still have that problem.

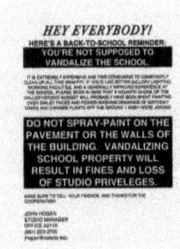

Hey Everybody! (Don't Vandalize The School) 2007, page 50
A rant, from a time when I felt it was important to explain every motivation for every decree to as many people as possible. Call it the grad school hangover. In my head, I was a put-upon everyman trying to make himself understood, but in hindsight, it's possible I was just being an asshole.

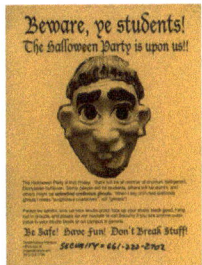

Beware, Ye Students! 2008, page 51
One year, in preparation for the Halloween Party, I created this poster at the request of the Security Committee, to promote awareness that creeps come to the campus and lurk around on Halloween. I think this was at a time when they didn't close down the entire school before the Halloween Party, as they do now.

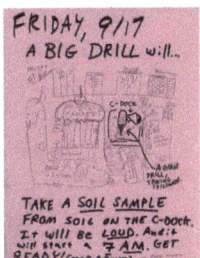

Big Drill (Pink) 2010, page 52
A construction crew needed to take a soil sample in an area close to many of the art studios. This area featured outdoor storage and a kind of liminal encampment for heshers and ne'er-do-wells that would feature occasional bonfires. According to CalArts lore, Neil Diamond played a concert at CalArts and donated his stage to the school, resulting in a lot of unused stage equipment with "NEIL DIAMOND" stenciled on it. We felt advance warning was needed before the drilling occurred.

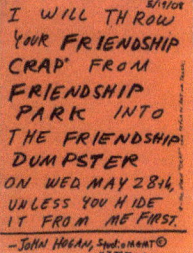

Friendship Crap 2008, page 53
This flyer was probably counterproductive, but it was a gratifying and cathartic experience to produce. "Friendship Park" was the name given by someone at some point to the raised "garden" in the Broad studios, which features sand, a tree, some rocks, and a tonnage of artistic debris.

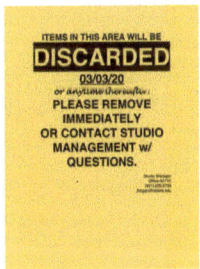

Discard Notice 2020, page 54
This is an example of a typical "Discard Notice" we leave when something needs to be moved or thrown away. It essentially puts objects "on notice."

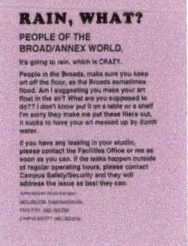

Rain, What? 2015, page 55
We had something like seven years of drought so whenever it would rain it was a catastrophe.

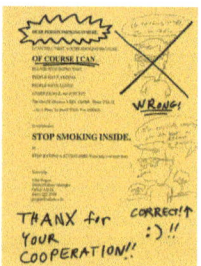

No Smoking (Be A Decent Person) 2012, page 56
Kind of obnoxious but I stand behind it 100%.

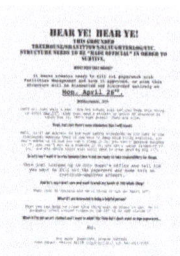

Hear Ye! Hear Ye! 2006, page 57
Some students made an elaborately titled fort out of garbage and the School of Art was advised that a student should formally claim it as their artwork or else it would be thrown away.

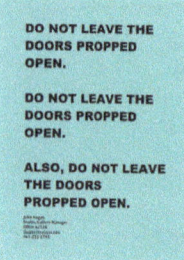

Do Not Leave The Doors Propped Open 2011, page 58
Many of the studios are in big shared rooms, or "studio blocks," with small locking studios that have walls you can climb over if you want to. Things get stolen and weirdos linger in halls, and fire-escape egress is obstructed if you prop the doors open with a trash can or a bottle of bleach or whatever.

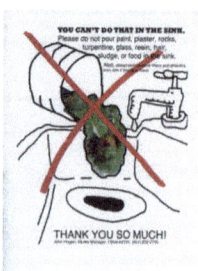

You Can't Do That... 2009, page 60
This flyer is a reference to (and contains imagery from) the Canadian 1980's children's show *You Can't Do That On Television*, in which members of the teenaged ensemble cast would have water dumped on their head if they said the word "water" and green slime dumped on their head if they said "I Don't Know." This flyer was meant to spread awareness of certain items that would be very harmful to dump into the sink, for health and environmental reasons.

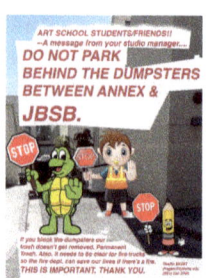

Don't Park By Dumpsters 2017, page 61
My first child was two years old when I had to make this flyer asking people not to park next to a building. The vibe of children's book illustrations and children's safety yielded this odd creation.

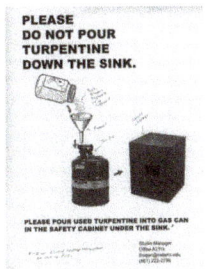

Turpentine Disposal Scheme 2015, page 62
Self-explanatory (and possibly deeply flawed) system I came up with for disposing of turpentine, as an alternative to pouring it down the sink and into our groundwater.

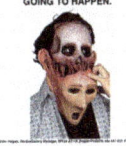

Scary Discard Notice 2013, page 63
Having previously not wanted to be scary, at some point I reversed course and endeavored to be totally scary when having to threaten to throw people's things away. I very much do not want to throw out someone's artwork by accident, for reasons both ethical and selfish, so I really tried to grab people by the collar here to let them know very bad things could happen if they didn't clean up their junk.

Please Do Not Draw... (Part One) 2018, page 64
It is a tricky proposition to make a sign admonishing graffiti artists. You need to expect that the sign will be defaced by the exact people you are telling not to deface things. It's an irresistable dare. It would seem like a fool's errand to bother making a notice at all, but if I didn't make an effort, all would descend into chaos.

Please Do Not Draw... (Part Two) 2018, page 66
I attempted to thwart my adversaries by actually writing a little note telling the graffitists not to engage in the most on-the-nose act of subversion (crossing out the "NOT" in "DO NOT DRAW, WRITE OR PAINT..."). In this case, I won the battle, but lost the war.

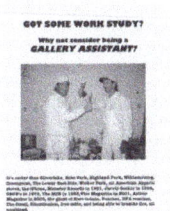

Got Some Work Study? 2009, page 67
This is a great sample of the cool things that I knew about, created exactly when I stopped knowing about cool things.

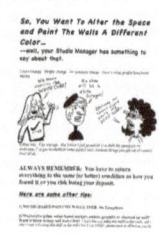
So, You Want To Alter The Space and Paint the Walls a Different Color... (Page One) 2008, page 68
A three page booklet distributed to BFA-1 students before their Foundation year show, to spread the word of all that is involved with painting a wall a weird color in one of the student galleries.

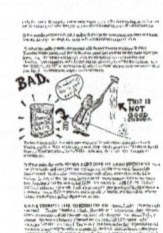
So, You Want To Alter The Space and Paint the Walls a Different Color... (Page Two) 2008, page 69

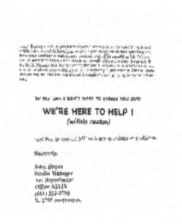
So, You Want To Alter The Space and Paint the Walls a Different Color... (Page Three) 2008, page 70

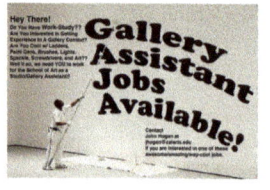
Gallery Assistant Jobs Available! (Painter) 2008, page 71

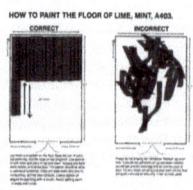
How To Paint the Floor 2018, page 71
My own staff needed serious guidance on how to paint the floor of a gallery. The people who work for me are usually only working over the weekend, so I had to resort to an inter-gallery-staff flier to convey the correct technique.

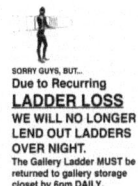

Ladder Loss 2009, page 72
This scheme to stop ladder theft did not work at all, regardless of whether or not I found an awesome jpeg of someone stealing a ladder in ski mask and heels.

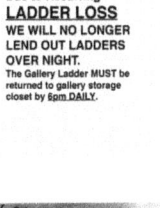

Paint Brush Poem 2009, page 73
This poem is pretty uncool, but I do continue to enjoy my own use of white-out-and-Sharpie-on-photocopy to accentuate the difference between a happy/clean paintbrush and a sad/dirty one.

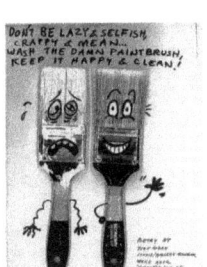

The Toilet Is Tired 2010, page 74
The toilet in one of the studio blocks was leaking constantly and I had been convinced by others with their own agenda that it was due to "overuse." Many years later this toilet continued to leak frequently, even while the studios were closed due to Covid-19, so the claims of toilet exhaustion seem unfounded.

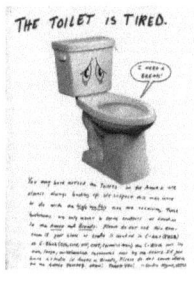

Santa Ana Winds 2019, page 75
There is a barbecue area with a built-in grill outside of a graduate-level studio block, created for the purposes of conviviality. It is not without potential for disaster.

Overspray 2008, page 76

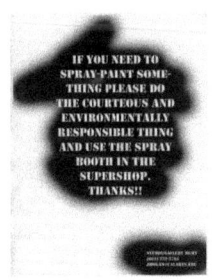

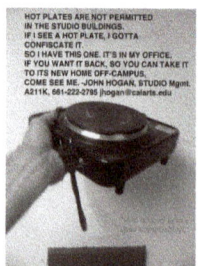

Hot Plates 2014, page 77

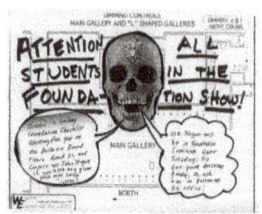

Crystal Skull 2008, page 78
This skull is Damien Hirst's *For The Love of God*, overlaid onto a map of the Main Gallery. At the time of this poster, Hirst's diamond-encrusted platinum-cast skull was the most expensive artwork to ever be produced.

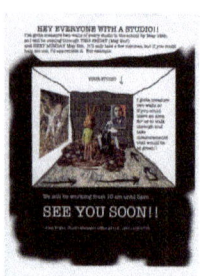

See You Soon, 2009 page 79
A personal favorite. The purpose of this flyer is so boring that I tried to make it interesting by packing it with a Sgt-Pepper-album-cover level of art and pop culture references.

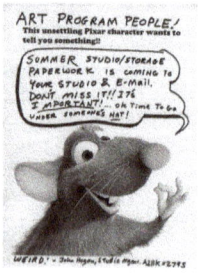

Ratatouille 2013, page 80
There is a big Pixar affiliation at CalArts, and I figured some animation students might take a second look at this, even though I didn't actually need them to read it. Anyway, I found Ratatouille uncanny, distressing and strange.

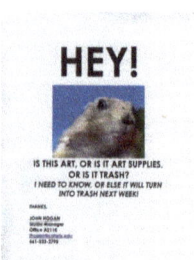

HEY! 2009, page 81
Dramatic Squirrel was all the rage when this flyer was put to print. I harnessed its popularity to raise awareness that I did not want to accidentally throw away art that I mistook for garbage.

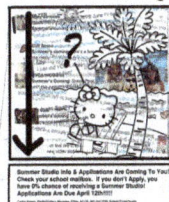

Summer's Coming! 2013, page 83
Over the summer, CalArts is taken over by CSSSA (the California State Summer School of the Arts), an arts camp for high school students. CSSSA takes over many studios and classrooms, and fills them with teens. To complicate things, we permit some CalArts students to stick around and make art. At the "Summer Info Sessions," I tell the college students if they want to stay, they must Keep Away From the Teens.

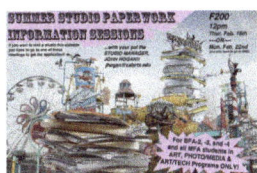

Summer Fun Fair 2016, page 84-85
The visual noise of absurdly large stacks of paperwork integrates almost too well with that of a carnival. This flyer is from a time when I distributed then collected a multi-page physical application and info sheet for summer studio access. There was even a second round of paperwork to distribute and collect for those who were accepted.

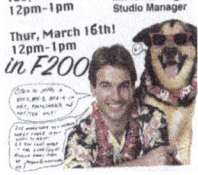

Summer Studio Info - Mark Harmon 2015, page 86

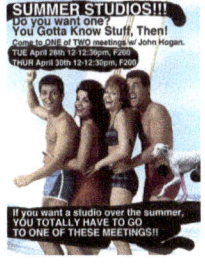

Beach Blanket Bingo 2010, page 87
The high-concept element of this otherwise boilerplate beach party scene is that Human, a dog with a leg dyed pink by Pierre Hyughe for his retrospective at LACMA, is acting as a Spuds McKenzie stand-in.

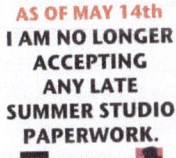

Mimes 2008, page 88
I don't know why I thought this would be coherent. A sad mime and a happy mime on a flyer saying I won't accept late paperwork. Why? Maybe to mock the idea of bringing me your sad stories for why it's late? I don't know, probably.

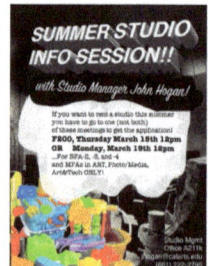

Beach Toy Brancusi 2016, page 89
Brancusi's studio and a bunch of summer sand toys.

Summer Studio Info - Animals 2019, page 90
Here's yet another Summer Studio Info Session flyer, encouraging students from various programs and year levels to convene and get their summer information from me. This flyer is inspired by the children's book *Night Tree*, which features a menagerie of wildlife circling around a wild Christmas tree decked with millet seed balls and popcorn strings.

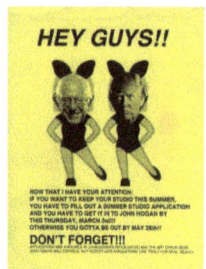

Studio Info - Hey Guys!! (Bernie & Trump) 2016, page 91

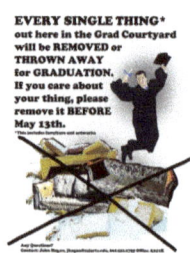

Couch Jumper 2008, page 92
There was a time when people really piled things up (especially couches) outside in an area that was used for the commencement ceremony. Sometimes these couches were dumpster finds, other times there'd be some claim that they were family heirlooms, so you have to give fair warning in no uncertain terms.

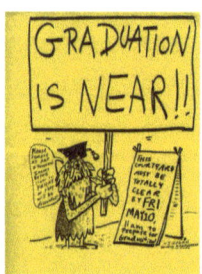

Graduation Is Near 2008, page 93
At the end of the year it's time to clean up and make way for graduation. There is often a lot of garbage that accumulates over the course of an academic year in the area where the graduation ceremony is held. This all has to be cleaned up and thrown away, which necessitates lots of flyers to warn people about what's going to happen.

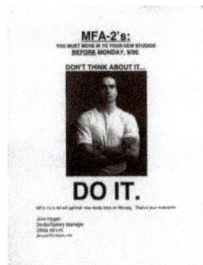

DO IT! 2011, page 95
I am not intimidating, but Henry Rollins is.

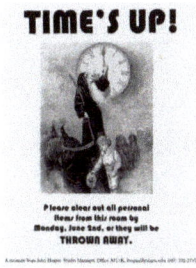

Time's Up 2009, page 96

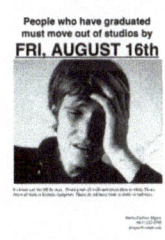

Move Out, Bas Jan Ader 2009, page 97
Pandering to the Conceptual Art Superfans is important when trying to get people to move out of places.

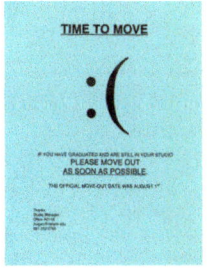

Time To Move :(2011, page 98
This is a move-out notice that is much softer in its approach, and which acknowledges text emoticons as a legitimate form of personal expression and communication.

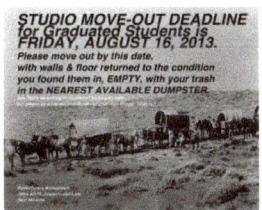

Wagon Train 2013, page 99
The imperialistic westward expansion of the United States was a catastrophe for native tribes, local wildlife and all those who died in the service of Manifest Destiny... lol.

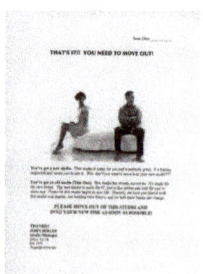

You Need To Move Out! 2007, page 100
This is a flyer addressing a specific problem: someone has been assigned a new studio, but has not moved out of their old studio. By now I have figured out ways of incentivizing the move, but in my early, unsophisticated years of studio management, I could rely on nothing but the applied, sustained pressure of caustic, barbed humor.

Grad Crit Room 2008, page 101
There is a room where the Graphic Design Program's MFAs have critiques, aptly referred to as the "Grad Crit Room." This room doubles as a storage room for students over the summer. Thus, the dirty sock.

Wilson 2013, page 103
This flyer was a collaboration with Taralyn Thomas.

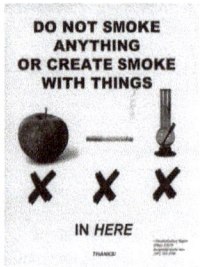

**Do Not Smoke Anything Or
Create Smoke With Things** 2013, page 104
This is a kind of collaboration with Magnus Maxine. I think we discussed the messaging and collaborated on the copy. I made some general illustrational suggestions, but Magnus made the final call regarding apple and bong imagery.

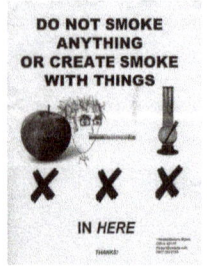

**Do Not Smoke Anything Or
Create Smoke With Things (Defaced)** 2013, page 105
People don't like being told not to smoke. These flyers often get defaced. I saved this particular one that looks to have a portrait of me on it.

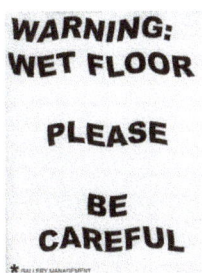

Warning: Wet Floor 2013, page 106
Can't remember why we made Wet Floor Warnings, but Bedros Yeretzian composed this piece and I find it very elegant.

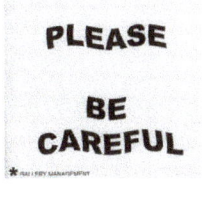

HEY MAN... 2013, page 107
A student was letting their dog pee in the corners of the hallways of the school. We were asked by Facilities to address this issue, somehow. Taralyn Thomas made this flyer, under my "art direction."

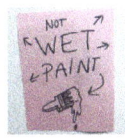

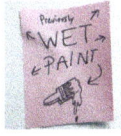

(NOT) WET PAINT
&
(Previously) WET PAINT 2019 page 108
I decided to make my own Wet Paint sign with a cartoon brush loaded with paint. Cute! But I forgot to take them down after the paint dried, so this sign became a collaborative work of art, as someone added "Not" and "Previously" to the tops of all the flyers. Meta!

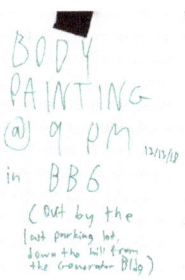

Streak Notice 1&2 by UNKNOWN, 2020, page 109-110

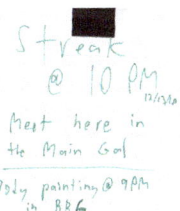

www.ingramcontent.com/pod-product-compliance
Lightning Source LLC
Chambersburg PA
CBHW040548220526
45473CB00017B/3051